NOR SHALL
MY SWORD

Also by the author

NOR SHALL MY SWORD

The Reinvention of England

SIMON HEFFER

Weidenfeld & Nicolson
LONDON

First published in Great Britain in 1999
by Weidenfeld & Nicolson

A CIP catalogue record for this book is available
from the British Library.

ISBN 0 297 64332 0

Typeset by Selwood Systems, Midsomer Norton

Set in Monotype Janson Text

Printed in Great Britain by Butler & Tanner Ltd, Frome and London

Weidenfeld & Nicolson
The Orion Publishing Group Ltd
Orion House
5 Upper Saint Martin's Lane
London, WC2H 9EA

In Memoriam

JAMES HEFFER

A Soldier of the Great War

CONTENTS

ACKNOWLEDGEMENTS

Miss Sally Chatterton, Professor Ian Campbell, Mrs Robert Rockall, Professor Anthony King, Benedict Brogan and The Scottish Office all provided or helped provide important factual material for me to use in writing this tract. Mr Matthew d'Ancona did me the conspicuous service of reading the manuscript and making some perceptive and enlightened observations upon it, for which I salute him. I should like to thank my editor, Ion Trewin, his assistant Miss Rachel Leyshon, my publisher Anthony Cheetham and my agent Miss Georgina Capel for their help and support. This book was my wife's idea, though all blame for what is found therein must attach to me.

Simon Heffer
Great Leighs
16 January 1999

ONE

A Crisis of Identity

Only the most unobservant can have missed the latest great fact in what the Victorians so charmingly called 'our island story': that a majority of the Scots wish to loosen their nation's antique ties with England. The point was spectacularly confirmed at the general election of 1 May 1997, when the main Unionist party in Scotland was unable to secure the return of a single candidate to the United Kingdom parliament at Westminster. The message was relayed even more loudly at the referendum on the Scottish parliament held in September 1997, when the Scots voted by a substantial majority to establish such a legislative body. At almost every opinion poll since then it has been shown that public support for the main separatist party in Scotland, the Scottish Nationalist Party, is growing steadily. In September 1998, exactly a year after the referendum, 50 per cent of Scots questioned in an opinion survey wanted their country to be independent. Another survey, taken three months earlier, made the more telling point that a majority of Scots, including many who do not wish for independence, nonetheless expect their country to be independent from England within about fifteen years.

The phenomenon of Scottish separatism is growing not least because among the young it has become a fashionable attitude. The glib explanation for why this should be so has for the last few years been that this generation was much moved by the film *Braveheart*, in which mediaeval Englishmen are seen brutalising, oppressing and generally being unsportsmanlike towards mediaeval Scotsmen. It may be that this fairly typical piece of Hollywood anti-Englishry acted as useful propaganda for the Scots nationalist cause, but that cause was already well advanced before Mr Mel Gibson lent his reputation to it, and for reasons that we shall shortly explain.

Whenever the movement really took off, it is now entrenched. An ICM survey carried out in Scotland for the *Scotsman* newspaper in June 1998 showed that 63 per cent of people in the eighteen to thirty-four age group would prefer to see Scotland as an independent country. The very mindset of the Scots about their place in the Union, their very expectations for the future, are being steadily revised and altered. It is not just that young people are being bombarded by propaganda in the media; they are growing up, in their families and their schools, imbued with the idea that the Union is detrimental to them, their freedoms, and their right to self-expression.

Those who feel this way have had other, broader sources of influence. Europe – in the true sense of that term – has only recently experienced a great flowering of nationalism. It is less than ten years since joyous Germans dismantled the Berlin Wall. Nations that existed only in the mind a decade ago – Slovakia, Slovenia, Estonia and the rest – are now literally on the map. Their renascence has helped change decades-old perceptions of nationalism. The two world wars meant that, to a modern audience, the concept smacked of aggression, domination and destruction, racialism and even genocide. Now, with the dismantling of the Soviet empire, nationalism is increasingly seen as representing something explicitly different: liberation from foreign control, social and economic freedom, decentralisation and cultural diversity. Even though the Scots have no recent history of suffering oppression – other than in the imaginations of some of the more eccentric of them – they have, in certain respects, latched on to the new public mood about nationalism, and in their aspirations are clearly benefiting from it. The sense of what Scottish nationalists seek to do is not the issue in this regard. A liberal nation like England should, and must, recognise the Scots' right to pursue their own identity, however costly a mistake it might prove for them.

If there is writing on Hadrian's Wall, it reads that the English should leave Scotland to its own devices. The subtext is that the Union of England and Scotland, which was made principally for economic reasons almost three hundred years ago, no longer confers sufficient benefit upon the Scots to make the sacrifice of their national independence worthwhile. It was in recognition of this mood, and in acknowledgement of the electoral considerations that hinge upon it, that the offer of devolution was made by a United Kingdom government. However, the measure of self-rule afforded to the Scots by devolution, with its limited tax-raising powers and lack of control over defence, foreign, employment, transport and other economic policies, is plainly not enough for the tastes and ambitions of many in Scotland. For the moment, this is a most one-sided debate: all the expression of grievance has been on the side of the Scots. It might be considered pointless now to have a referendum in England about whether that country should – irrespective of what Scotland tries or decides to do – become independent, however much the English might deserve the sort of consideration that has already been given to the Scots and the Welsh, and however unintentionally amusing the exercise might be. There is no reason why it should not take two to make an independence movement; there is no reason not to ask the English whether or not they would like to be shot of the Scots, although the Scots appear to have reached that point first. Sadly, this basic democratic right will not be afforded to the English. In the drama that may be about to unfold, they must accept, it seems, the role of the completely passive partner. That is only the first, but most fundamental, way in which the English have been betrayed by the political class of all parties that claims to govern them in their interests.

Should the SNP form an administration after the elections to the 129-seat Scottish parliament, to be held on 6 May 1999, its programme is clear. At its heart is a promise of a referendum on whether to maintain the Union with England. That plebiscite would, according to the SNP, happen during the new parliament's first fixed four-year term. The probability is that it would not occur until towards the end of that period, so it is likely to be 2002 before such a choice is put to the Scottish people. As we have increasingly seen with referenda here and abroad – whether for the signing up of Denmark to the Maastricht Treaty, or over such vital issues as whether women should be allowed to join the Marylebone Cricket Club – such ballots tend to be held again and again until the 'right' result is obtained. Indeed, that is exactly how devolution for Scotland - the start of the independence process – was brought about in the first place. When the Scots and Welsh were last asked about this subject, in March 1979, the Welsh rejected it outright and the Scots accepted the notion, but by a majority insufficiently large to enable the changes to be carried through. Should the SNP be in a position to call a plebiscite, and should the result not please it, one can expect the process to be embarked upon again. The issue of Scottish independence smacks of being one that will not be put to rest until the goal is achieved. Indeed, it may be only by being independent that Scotland realises what a bad idea – for the Scots – the notion really is.

It has taken the English some time to start to understand the phenomenon of Scottish separatism. Indeed, it is apparent that many of them do not understand it yet. Only the more historically minded will sense that the country has travelled a similar road before, in all the arguments about Irish home rule since the middle of the nineteenth century. Then, it was argued by conservatives of all parties that a vicious blow would be struck not just to the integrity of the Kingdom, but of what was then the British Empire, if the Irish were allowed to rule themselves, even under the British Crown. Now, it can be seen that one of the greatest mistakes in modern British history was the failure of parliament in 1886 to pass Gladstone's Home Rule Bill, and to accept the natural consequences of full independence that would, one day, have flowed from that in a democracy. A lesson has, or should have, been learned that when a mature and discrete section of people within a modern state wish to reserve their democratic destiny to themselves, there is nothing to be gained by preventing them. If a clear majority of the Scots should at some time wish to emulate the Irish of the twenty-six counties, only a fool would seek to stop them. It may well be that the Scots would harm themselves economically, socially and diplomatically by doing so. That, sadly, must be their lookout if they choose to ignore the apparently compelling arguments that should reinforce the idea of Union. The cost to the English of keeping them from such harm would be far more than the cost of allowing them, like all grown-up people, to make their own mistakes and to take whatever follows from those mistakes.

One of the numerous failures of leadership in Britain in recent years has been the reluctance of our governors, and those who think for them, to accept the new realities about the future of the Union. This has been as apparent in the context of the effects of devolution as it has been in the matter of the Scots' desire for separatism. The contradiction of a part of the Kingdom's having two parliaments, as is about to be the case with Scotland, was first highlighted by the Labour MP Tam Dalyell during the debates on the Scotland Bill in 1977. Taking the name from his own constituency, Mr Dalyell framed 'the West Lothian Question'. He asked: why should the representative from West Lothian (or any other Scottish constituency, for that matter) be able to sit in the Westminster parliament and vote on parochial matters affecting the English, when the English Members who sat in the same parliament were entirely unable to vote on parochial matters affecting the Scots, for those matters were now to be considered by Scotland's own parliament?

In a style that has become more familiar with the growing intensity of national decline, many in the political class pretended that Mr Dalyell's pertinent and important question did not matter. The attitude was, more often than not, that it would serve the English right, as some sort of part-repayment for their centuries of interference in the affairs of the Scots; or, simply, that it would not make any difference. However, many people, including some at the highest level not just of what was then the Government but of what was then the (Conservative) Opposition, recognised that, inevitably, it did matter: but they were never going to own up to that. The principle appeared to be that what the English eye did not see, the English heart could not grieve over. Labour wanted devolution to keep its own sizeable support in Scotland sweet: the Conservatives, relatively well represented in Scotland in that era long before Mr Major had led them to apocalypse, wanted to devise a measure of devolution compatible with their own instinctive, atavistic, sentimental desire for the political and constitutional unity of Great Britain. The cack-handed, muddle-headed abortion of logic that became the Conservative plans for devolution in the 1970s were supported even by Mrs Thatcher herself, then Leader of the Opposition. Defeatist as ever, the Conservatives generally accepted that the Scots would vote for devolution; it was equally feared by both main parties that if they did, any attempt to take the West Lothian Question to its correct – and devastatingly separatist – conclusion would be fatal for the Union that both parties, for their different reasons, wished to maintain. A conspiracy of silence, not entirely successful, sprang up on the issue.

As we have noted the Scots did, in March 1979, vote for devolution: but by an insufficient majority to allow the proposals to be implemented. For the eighteen years of Conservative rule that followed, the Government tried to appease devolutionist and separatist opinion in various non-legislative ways, mainly by spraying vast amounts of English taxpayers' money over the Scots and Scotland, and occasionally by sending

Mrs Thatcher on imperial visits to Caledonia to attempt to be nice to the natives. A cultural chasm opened up: the alienation of the English by the Scots became rampant. The Labour party (which would, in time, suffer from the effects of this chasm almost as much as the Conservatives) began to step up its own insistence on devolution. Slowly, and for a long time barely perceptibly, the proportions of Scots who were devolutionists and those who were separatists began to shift. The latter grew in numbers at the expense of the former. The English, first saturated in money after the deregulations and speculations of the 1980s, and then cut off at the knees by the economic mismanagement of Nigel Lawson and John Major, were alternately too selfish and then too immersed in their own miseries to bother very much about what was happening in Scotland. That was partly why there was such shock when the Conservatives were wiped out in 1997: at last, Scotland had been heard loud and clear.

Labour's success in that election – in which they won fifty-six of the country's seventy-two seats – was partly a tribute to the Scots' hatred of Mr Major and his weak, unprincipled, gutless and predominantly (but not exclusively) English cohorts. It was more, though, a signal that the Scots wished to vote for a party that would spur through devolution and (though this was not appreciated at the time by the Labour party) allow them, before too long, to choose whether or not they would ever again need to submit to rule by buffoons and charlatans from another country. Labour was utterly unequivocal in its manifesto pledges about devolution. The Scots, shrewdly, realised that by electing them they would get the first measure of power they needed: they could then switch allegiance to a party that promised not just devolution (which would, by then, already have been accomplished) but full-blown separatism. For Labour not to have realised that this was the plan betrays a stunning naïveté.

It was apparent to most people before the 1997 election that

7

(a) Labour would win it and form a government for the first time in eighteen years and (b) that their commitment to devolution, stalled just before the first of their four electoral defeats, would be demonstrated without delay. The debate about devolution conducted during the 1990s, under Conservative rule, was therefore not merely theoretical or speculative. It is regrettable, therefore, that it was conducted in so unreal a fashion.

Labour's commitment, while in opposition, to a Scottish parliament was clear. Equally clear were the Conservative party's objections to such a course. Clinging to their romantic and sentimental Unionism despite categorical evidence that few intelligent (or, for that matter, unintelligent) people in Scotland felt the same way, the Conservatives never tried to dictate the terms of the debate. Nor did they really succeed in forcing Labour to defend its position on devolution. There was one obvious way in which the Conservatives could have sought to do this, but it entailed the sort of original approach to the question and the sort of aggressive gambling that the party was simply not prepared to consider during the Major years. As such, it can now be seen that its survival in office was set above the survival of the Union. More painfully, the worst outcome of the gamble it refused to take could well yet result anyway.

The gamble would have been for the Conservative Party to say, as early as at the 1992 election, the following. It could have stated that it recognised the mounting desire for some sort of home rule in Scotland. It could have added that, as a democratic party, it had no intention of ignoring the will of the Scottish people on this question. Therefore, it was going to take the initiative, and offer a choice in the matter. However, it would not and could not be the type of choice that the Labour party had in mind, for their notions were entirely unrealistic and deeply unfair to the great majority of people in the United Kingdom – that is to say, the English.

Labour envisaged the creation of a parliament in Edinburgh whose principal function in life would be to lobby to prise more and more money out of the English. Furthermore, it would be a parliament that gave Scotland and the Scots various advantages over the English which, in a free and equal Union, would lead to manifest unfairness. This unfairness would extend beyond the failure to answer the West Lothian Question. As with independence movements the world over, a parliament with limited functions would be likely to become the power base for a separatist movement – or, indeed, the very Trojan horse in which such a movement was introduced to the front rank of Scottish politics. Therefore, the Conservatives might have said, we are going to stop messing about, and short-circuit the whole process.

They could then have announced that their choice would focus the debate on the only viable long-term alternatives for Scotland: to stay as it was within the Union, governed from Westminster with a Secretary of State, a Grand Committee and the rest, accepting the legislation of the British parliament and the rule of the British government; or to have complete independence, legislating for and ruling itself. For reasons of fairness to the English, and recognising what was likely to be the evolving nature of Scottish opinion once a devolved parliament was set up, the indefinite existence of such a devolved parliament, contentedly (from either the Scottish or English point of view) working within the remit set by Westminster, was highly improbable.

Such a debate would have caused examination of the realities in a way that has never yet taken place. The interesting assertions of the Scottish Nationalist Party about, in particular, Scotland's prospects as an independent economic entity would have been scrutinised and tested in a way that has not yet occurred in a British context, and may now only happen in a Scottish one. If the devolved parliament had never been an option – provided it had been clearly explained why, in everybody's best interests, it could not be an option – the apparently easy course for the Scots of discarding the Union would never have been there. In the context of six or seven years ago, such a debate might have brought home to the Scots that, however much they hated a Conservative government (a sentiment in which they were joined, daily, by an increasing number of the English), they were better off staying in the Union on the prevailing terms. As these terms included better representation in parliament per head than the English, and more public spending per head too – not to mention international participation in forums such as the G8, the European Union, NATO and (for what it is worth) the United Nations – it was hardly as if the Scots were being ripped off.

However, the question was never put to them in those terms. Instead, Scotland has voted for its devolved parliament, and the process of full independence has been set in train. As the people of England, who often give the unfortunate appearance of being complacent, slow-witted and uninterested in politics, witness this phenomenon from the other side of the border, even they are being stirred to some resentment. Thanks to the cause being taken up by various English newspapers, increasing numbers of the English are now well aware of what Scotland costs them, and that it has better parliamentary representation per head of the population (a legacy of the terms of the Act of Union) than, say, Essex or Lancashire. They cannot see why this should be the case. Moreover, when they hear the likes of the leader of the Scottish Nationalist Party declaim his right to govern himself, they interpret him – whatever his phraseology might have been – as voicing an anti-English sentiment. Something stirs deep in the blood of the English. The whole notion stimulates, and offends, their atavistic sense of fair play and decency. It may all be a horrible misunderstanding, but the opinion polls from Scotland only seem to confirm the message of the inevitability of separation. So, finally, the English end up feeling that if the Scots want to be rid of England, then maybe it is not, after all, such a good idea for the English to cling on to the Scots.

II

That sort of thinking by the English is, however, part of a process that is only now slowly getting under way. There is still, for the most part, incomprehension at the prospect that England and Scotland could once more, after nearly three hundred years in the Union and having shared a monarchy for almost four hundred, become separate states. We speak, after a fashion, the same language. We share the same institutions, from the Queen downwards. We all play soccer, drink beer and whisky, watch *Coronation Street* and, in relatively large numbers, live in each other's countries. However, the English (unlike their Scottish cousins) are a simple and politically unsophisticated people. Therefore, it is often the case that they cannot understand that separatism might happen because they still cannot see any need why it should have to happen. As far as the English are concerned, the Scots are not being oppressed by them. They have democratic institutions and benefit greatly from the spending of British revenue. More to the point, since May 1997 a third of the Cabinet has been Scottish. Why on earth should these people be so dissatisfied with the Union that they should feel a need to get out of it? If the English – easy-going and complacent as ever – were in the same position, they would find nothing to complain about. Moreover, it is a paradox of the Anglo-Scottish relationship of late that while the Scots have devoted much of their intellectual and emotional energy to thoughts about England, the English have – until very recently – devoted almost none at all of theirs to thoughts about Scotland. This might not have mattered so much if those Scottish thoughts had been ones of affection, admiration and satisfaction; but they have not.

For the English, history is not much of a help here either. They cannot comprehend today the forces of Scottish separatism nearly so well as they just about understood those of

Irish separatism in the 1880s. There is not the geographical divide with Scotland, sharing as the two countries do a land border, nor is there the important cultural difference of religion. Equally, though, it is hard to see what the English now have to fear from fragmentation of the Union – certainly not so much as their great-grandfathers feared a century ago. No imperial power or integrity is at stake; and the idea of a united kingdom is just another one of those constitutional notions that the English feel they instinctively care about – so well indoctrinated have they been – but for which they are hard put to mount anything other than a sentimental defence, the defence that 'well, it has always been there'. Scotland, with its five million people out of a United Kingdom total of 58 million, would only be a marginal loss to England, and no loss at all in economic terms. England would still be as much of a power in the European Union and in NATO as Britain was before it. Its permanent place on the United Nations Security Council is not dependent on the Union with Scotland; similarly, losing the financial drain of Scotland is hardly likely to eliminate it from the club of the G8. Scotland would have none of these things except (it hopes) membership of the EU as a minor statelet, with commensurately little influence. That, as we have noted, is up to the Scots. Those English who believe in the Union can make their forceful arguments about the benefits to Scotland of staying in; but should the Scots decide to leave, their destiny need not concern the English, any intervention by whom at that time would rank as an intrusion into private grief.

For the moment, though, the English need to be very much concerned about what is going on in Scotland. What that country may be about to do, by empowering the Scottish Nationalist Party in the 1999 elections, is something even the English ought to have woken up to a little more than they have. Unfortunately, it is in the English bloodstream not to notice, or care about, such things. This regrettable trait has become more embedded as the twentieth century has worn on, with the

English people exhausted by two world wars, cushioned by what they interpret as prosperity and corrupted by welfarism. Not having been oppressed by a foreign power since 1066, not having had a bloody revolution, and not lately having had to fight for a say in who runs their country, the English are content to maintain their great uninterest in politics. High constitutional questions that so vex commentators, academics and the political class seem rarely to register with the English general public. They would much rather worry about something else, such as the lives of characters in their favourite soap operas, or the fortunes of their favourite soccer team; concerns they believe, possibly rightly, also affect their cousins in Scotland. What they do not see is that many Scots, as well as having those shared concerns, have room in their mental wardrobes to think about how they are governed, and why they are governed in the way that they are. The English, or almost all of them, lack that capacity, or the stimulus to it. If they had, some of the abominations perpetrated against Britain in the interests of European Union since the passage of the 1972 European Communities Act would never have been allowed to happen.

It is, therefore, likely to come as something of a shock to the English if they wake up one morning, not many years hence, and discover that the country they have lived in all their lives has, by the will of another people, had its boundaries radically altered. Such geographical and political upheaval would not be the end of it, however. It would pose to the English a question that in the interests of their national survival and coherence would have to be answered, and which they could only answer themselves: who, after all this time in their Union with Scotland, do they think they are?

The English – a term which, for these purposes, we must understand as including all those who inhabit the land of England – have (for various reasons that we shall encounter) tended more than is good for them to think of themselves as British. That is to say, in many contexts they have thought of themselves as British if they have to think of themselves as anything at all. This may well be a sign that they take the Union for granted, and as defining them. For the Scots, for some years now, the Union has been something about which they constantly think, and for which they continually have had to make accommodations with their instinctive Scottishness. It is still remembered with rancour in Scotland that the Scots were forced to style the present Queen Elizabeth II, even though they had had no Elizabeth I. In this, though the English may not have realised it then, or even realise it now, the Scots taught them a valuable lesson about identity. The lesson is that it is perverse for people who live and have roots in an old country not to identify themselves explicitly with that country, whatever the apparent incentives may be to do otherwise.

It is, however, a perversity in which the English, who have a national characteristic of taking much for granted, happily and deeply indulge. It is not at all surprising that their Britishness should in many respects be so far in advance of their Englishness. The Victorians, in particular, put so much effort into creating a British culture, iconography, symbolism and nation that such an assault on the senses is bound to take several generations to fade away: but fade it will. The English, and whatever they feel to be Englishness, are and always have been far and away the main contributors to Britain and Britishness. Those English who have made the effort of self-identification, therefore, all too easily identify themselves as British – or at least, until the devolution question raised the profile of the issue, they did. The great exception to this rule seems to be when the English are following a sport: the England soccer team has done more to promote an English national identity in recent years (not inevitably healthily) than almost anything else. Such an interpretation of national identity remains the exception. The English may, though, soon find that they suddenly, and without much preparation, have to think of themselves as something altogether different from being British;

though in practice their new identity would be something very similar, if not identical, to the one they currently have.

If the English have only limited awareness that they are English, the Scots and Welsh have no such restricted self-knowledge. Only among Ulster Unionists, where the reasons for self-awareness are different, special, and steeped in the potent forces of blood and religion, does the label of 'British' (for the majority) supersede all else. The Scots and the Welsh too, in time of war during this century, have clearly and nobly seen themselves as British. However, as the generations that participated in those great national enterprises recede into the distance, so too does the consciousness of Britishness. If this were not so, there would be no separatist movements in those parts of what are, still, the United Kingdom.

It is one of the stupidities, or carelessnesses, of the English that they have for generations been so unaware of the quite legitimate self-regard of their neighbours in these islands. That self-regard perhaps explains the ferocious patriotism with which the non-English set out, in the nineteenth century, on the building of an Empire for Britain that was controlled from England; or, in this century, why they fought so bravely and self-sacrificingly in those wars embarked upon principally by the English in the name of Britain. Thanks, perhaps, to the campaign of terror that has been the latest manifestation of the ancient conflict between England and Ireland, even the English could not have missed the fact that the Irish, other than the Ulster Unionists, had a strong sense of their national identity. Yet if the English have noticed that the Scots think of themselves principally as Scottish, and the Welsh only a little less profoundly think of themselves as Welsh, the English have been slow to understand the full consequences of what such self-identification means. It means, of course, that the motive force of a nationalist movement in each of those countries is already in place, and that in the eyes of many in those parts of the Kingdom the English have become dispensable. The people of England have quite some ground to make up before they are equally ready to think of themselves instinctively and naturally as English.

III

So far we have focused on Scotland, because it is there that a democratic and constitutional separatist movement has its best head of steam, and where it is most speedily likely to be challenging for power. It is from there that the Union faces its greatest threat: and, given the ancient status of Scotland as a nation and the relative size of its population, its secession from the Union would render the Union (even if the Welsh and the Northern Irish were still communicating members of it) unrecognisable by present standards. In law, of course, the secession of Scotland should not affect those other two parts of the realm. Wales was absorbed into the English state over four hundred years before the Act of Union; Northern Ireland's status was uncomfortably settled, separately, eighty years ago, though it could well be under threat again in the light of the 1998 Good Friday Agreement; time will tell. However, the English, when talking about the Union, have never restricted that notion to Scotland, but have used the term (with mild legal inaccuracy) to refer to the whole United Kingdom.

Northern Ireland and Wales have their own separatist movements, Northern Ireland infamously so. There, it is not just the predominantly Catholic nationalists and Republicans who would like to be sundered from Great Britain, in their case to be reunited with the Irish Republic. There are some Unionists in Ulster who would like an independent Six Counties, ruled from Belfast, perhaps under the British Crown, but certainly with no attachment to the English parliament. They feel that the future of Ulster as a Protestant state can be guaranteed only by themselves, something the attitudes of successive British – mainly Conservative – governments have given them every cause to believe. These Unionists are, however, very much in a minority. Most Ulster Protestants fear an independent Six Counties as being the first step in a process that would lead to reunification with the Irish republic. Once the tie with London is cut, they fear, the road to reunification would be cleared of its most important existing obstacles. It is, therefore, a great paradox that the movement among Protestants for such an independent state is motivated by the certain belief that London is insincere about protecting their tradition in the Six Counties, about maintaining their links to the Crown, and keeping Dublin's nose out of Northern Irish affairs.

The same argument about choosing between direct rule or independence that the English, as the dominant party in the Union, ought to offer the Scots cannot be put to the people of the Six Counties. Scotland's differences with England are not rooted in cancerous and inflammatory religious bigotry. In that regard those differences are more civilised, though less understandable by the very nature of their being differences between two very similar peoples. There is no element of violence or blood-hatred in them, though that could well change, as it has elsewhere in Europe, if the Scots were to be refused national self-determination. Between England and Scotland the problem is that the Scots have, once more, started to perceive themselves as a nation, which in historical terms they have every right to do. Whether or not they are a viable nation does not, for the moment, enter into it: nationalism is a potent, visceral force. Denying it is like denying human nature. Only a few superior, and somewhat unreal, beings can claim to be above it, and it is unwise that they should ever be encouraged to think that they speak for many others in holding such views.

The Six Counties are not a nation. About 40 per cent of those living there think they belong to a nation from which they are separated by a land border invented less than eighty years ago and unprotected by ancient precedent. The other 60 per cent think they belong to the British nation from which they are separated by a few miles of inhospitable water. That has been the cause of much of the trouble in those parts, reinforced by the melancholy tradition of violence and murder as a means of achieving political ends: a tradition that, many in the Republican movement might conclude after the Good Friday Agreement of 1998, has served them well. As the English should view it, the Six Counties cannot be regarded like the Scots: they are the rump of a colony which, ideally, would be integrated into the United Kingdom and ruled in the same manner as any other part of that kingdom. However, the security situation, and the historic lack of will by the British to enforce their rule in Ulster in accordance with the democratically expressed wishes of the majority there, means that such an option is not available to them. If the rights of that majority are to be upheld, along with its wish to remain loyal to the Crown, then the new arrangements for governing Ulster through its assembly, with its first minister and its element of devolution while retaining representation at Westminster, appears to be necessary. It is illogical and inequitable in the terms of the rest of the kingdom; but it also serves as an example of what happens in a polity such as ours when hard choices are shirked over a period of decades, when democratic logic is ignored and undermined, when politicians deceive themselves, when the will fails, and when realities are ignored. For the moment, in Ulster's highly volatile and barely peaceable state, there is little more that Britain can do by way of constitutional or political experiment there. The British people, on both sides of the Scottish border, should however reflect on the lesson Ulster teaches, and be determined not to let their own relationships degenerate in a similar way that necessitates a similarly unsatisfactory solution. They should also bear in mind the message that Scots independence might send to the people of Ulster, and whether – despite the absence of exact parallels – such a development might destabilise the Province once more. If Scottish independence cannot be stopped, then English politicians will have a duty to explain to Ulster and to the world – not least America – why Ulster is, and must remain, different.

The Welsh, with their assembly and representation at Westminster, might think of themselves as being in a similar position to the Northern Irish. However, their constitutional arrangements have been established out of political convenience, not as a matter of life and death. Welsh nationalism is a paltry operation, not least because of the incomprehension with which even many in Wales regard the concept of a Welsh nation. For many years it seemed as though Welsh nationalism (we must flatter the Welsh by using this nonsensical term) were restricted just to those whose identification with Wales was expressed in the extreme form of using the Welsh tongue. However in September 1998 Plaid Cymru, the Welsh nationalist party, sought (somewhat controversially) to broaden its appeal by adding to its name the English words 'the party of Wales', appropriately reflecting the fact that 80 per cent of those who live in Wales do not speak Welsh. This sort of thing invites a brief consideration of what Wales is, and what it historically has been.

Wales's absorption into the English state at the end of the thirteenth century is by now so entrenched that few in the principality seem to wish to attempt to dissolve it or, if they do, to know where and how to begin the process. The grave doubts that exist about whether Scotland could function on its own as an independent state, even one funded generously from Brussels, are nothing compared with those that must accompany any Welsh fantasies on the subject. There is a general recognition of this. When the devolution goodies came to be dished out by the victorious Labour government in 1997, Scotland was offered a parliament with some tax-raising powers. Wales was offered an assembly that would, in England, pass for a superior sort of county council. It was, as we have already noted, approved in the referendum of September 1997 by the smallest of margins; and that on a turnout of barely half the electorate. With about a quarter of Welsh adults supporting the new arrangements, there is no way in which the full-hearted consent of the people of Wales could be said to exist for devolution, let alone for independence.

Welsh nationalism is a preposterous concept because there is no Welsh nation. What was absorbed by the English after 1282 were separate little kingdoms and chiefdoms of the sort that had gone to make up England before the coming of the Normans. The Normans made England into a nation; the English made Wales into a coherent appendage of England's. Acts of Union in 1536 and 1543 formalised and regularised a position that had then existed for nearly two and a half centuries. The Welsh themselves, to judge from the half-hearted way in which they have always approached questions of devolution, have been among the first to see the somewhat fantastic nature of trying to unpick or dissolve arrangements as ancient as these. Also, if it is true that Wales as we understand it today is an English invention, Scotland manifestly is not. When the Welsh finally voted by the narrowest of margins in September 1997 to have even an assembly of highly circumscribed powers, they were hardly making a dragon's roar of nationalist fervour. If the choice offered to the Scots by the Labour government was muddle-headed, it was at least offered in response to a genuine nationalist movement, and in a doomed attempt to placate it. In Wales there was no such movement worthy of the name, no such recent and established tradition of nationalism to draw upon, no distinct survivals of an old Welsh nation from which to rekindle nationalist embers (in the way that the Scots have their legal and educational systems). For Labour, it was an act not so much wrong as pickled in cynicism; and some might argue that the embarrassments over who would be Labour's First Secretary candidate, when one incumbent resigned and another had to be parachuted in in the winter of 1998–9, were categorical proof of the existence of God. In any case, devolution guaranteed, in the absence of such nationalist feeling as exists in Scotland, a new tier of Labour-dominated government in a country that simply does not need it. Moreover, it provides it partly at English expense, despite the English taxpayer's not having been consulted on the matter.

The English, who we have noted are not the sharpest nor the most outward-looking of people, can be forgiven for being a little mystified about Wales. Not only does the present inadequate historical curriculum in schools not teach the important facts about how these parts of the kingdom came to be united; they have not been taught for some time. There have been other, minor episodes of confusion, such as the fact that so many people in Monmouthshire cannot seem to decide whether they are English or Welsh. While we can grasp the fact that Scotland once had its own kings, systems of government and institutions, and that at the definite date of 1707 it joined England in a Union, Wales just seems to have been there all along. To anyone with some education, it simply seems that Wales was incorporated in the English state in much the same way, and not very much later than the same time, as Wessex, Mercia, Cornwall or any of the other ancient and disparate sections of England were. If one day a parliament governing Wessex should once more sit in a village outside Salisbury, then that might be the time when the English concede and admit that parliaments for the ancient divisions of what is now Wales, and the attendant aspirations of Welsh nationalism, might be justifiable. What is more, it might take so drastic a dissolution of the English nation to provoke many of the Welsh to agree with them.

IV

There should, however, be no such lack of respect by the English concerning the legitimacy of the nationalist aspirations of the Scots. Scotland is a nation, or at least thinks it is, which is most of what is required to make it one. (That the Welsh, similarly, appear to have no such conception of themselves, but have instead most of what is required to think of themselves as a distinct region, is another reason why nationalism and Wales go so badly together.) Scotland's history, identity, culture, and definition are distinct. It had a separate existence until 1707, and for much of the century before that had lent England its kings. It is no colony, and – if it ever entertained one – it has shaken off the notion that it was some sort of client state of England's, entirely dependent upon England for its existence. (Of course, in fact Scotland is economically greatly dependent on England, but we shall deal with that later.) Thomas Carlyle, born in 1795 and raised just a few miles north of Gretna Green, may frequently have spoken of 'the English' as including himself, just as many educated Scots of his day did. Those, however, were the high days of Victorian imperialism, when it was the English–British identity that ruthlessly stamped itself all over the globe, even when it was Scots who (more often than not) did the stamping. That era has well and truly passed.

The Scots and the Welsh these days never confuse 'British' and 'English'. It causes much resentment, especially in Scotland, when the English do (I am reminded by Mr Matthew d'Ancona of the effects of Mr Michael Heseltine's observation in 1996 that there were 'distinguished Scots' in 'the English cabinet'): and quite right too. The ICM survey for the *Scotsman* newspaper in June 1998, carried out in Scotland, found that 59 per cent of those polled felt either 'more Scottish than British' or 'Scottish, not British': an increase of 11 per cent since the question had been asked in March 1997. The antipathy of the Scots to the notion of Britishness, we may assume, reflects a feeling that to be British means associating oneself too closely with the culture and institutions of the English. Nor do the majority in the Six Counties of Ulster who wish to remain tied to the British Crown tend to confuse their labels. The English themselves, however, are far less careful with their use of terminology. Partly for that reason, the English all too often have that interesting and, for them, uniquely depressing answer to the question 'who do you think you are?'; that they are British. This is not too surprising, for they are repeatedly told that they are just that. They read on their passports that it is the national identification naturally, and legally, attaching to them. Those who have migrated to England from overseas have become British, not English, citizens, for there is no legally based English citizenship. Their Government, and the Crown in whose name it rules, are British. For many who live in England and who are indeed entirely of English descent, 'British' is simply a synonym for 'English'; which, of course, it is not, despite the predominant contribution England and English culture have made to Britain and British culture.

This misunderstanding, or failure to think precisely, is unfortunate, on many counts. Soon, if the movement for Scottish nationalism continues to take its logical course, Britain will be just a geographical, and not a political, fact. For much of 1998, the last complete calendar year in which Scotland was ruled entirely by what some Ulstermen still lovingly call the 'imperial parliament' in London, the Scottish Nationalist Party ran Labour neck-and-neck in the opinion polls in Scotland. An English Prime Minister (albeit one born and educated in Scotland) faced an unpleasant, and growing, likelihood that his plans for devolution in Scotland might be about to go horribly wrong. The original idea had been that the Scots, grateful for being allowed their own parliament in Edinburgh, would in return happily elect a Labour administration there. This administration would be, in effect, a puppet regime of the Labour administration in London, which still retained a certain amount of power over United Kingdom issues such as defence and foreign policy. The English Labour Prime Minister would have his own placeman, a loyal member hitherto of his own British cabinet, presiding like a viceroy over the contented Scots. As we have seen, such a cosy arrangement was all very easy to impose upon the obliging Welsh, who are not really a nation, and who therefore willingly accept such patronage and favour in the same way that the Belgians have negated what little there was of themselves anyway and taken so much from the European Union. The ignorance of human nature, of history, of contemporary politics, and of decolonisation processes the world over that was revealed by Labour's belief that the Scots, too, would go along with this ruse without a fight was, however, staggering.

That ignorance is now being cruelly exposed. If, in May 1999, the Scots give the SNP some measure of power, one of two things will eventually happen. Either the SNP will prove so inept at exercising power (helped, one can be sure, by a not completely cooperative Labour government in London) that with the decline of its credibility it will be forced to abandon all hope of achieving complete independence, and it will lose office, perhaps for a generation, at the second Scottish elections. The future then would be uncertain and could only be judged in the context in which it would come about: there would be no certainty that Labour, the architects of devolution, would be rewarded for their mistake by being asked by the Scots to govern instead. Or, the SNP would govern in what the people of Scotland regarded as their best interests, bringing the clamour for a referendum on independence from England to a deafening pitch within a few years. It is hard to see a halfway house between these two extremes being sustained for long. When and if the SNP obtain power, even if (as is likely) it would have to be a minority government, it would take a leaf from New Labour's book and govern in opposition to some of its wilder instincts in order to hold onto power and to achieve its fundamental aim. The people who would elect the SNP would not do so in order for it not to proceed with independence, and to proceed with it speedily.

In one respect, the Labour government had no choice but to follow the course it has. It had promised – or rather the present

Prime Minister's predecessor as leader of the Labour party, John Smith, had promised – that devolution would be one of the commitments of the next Labour government. Mr Smith was a Scotsman, but one who enjoyed strutting on the English stage, and brought much colour and merriment to it. Unlike much of what Labour had stood for during the Smith years, this particular matter of principle survived into the party's 1997 manifesto. It was of a piece with the rest of the party's constitutional policy in that it was inadequately thought through, and its consequences remained miraculously invisible to those in charge of prosecuting it, even though many other politicians and commentators saw the dangers brightly illuminated, and did not keep their vision to themselves. All one can suppose is that, when so much else was being jettisoned from Labour's hot air balloon, it was considered soothing to keep something to remind people of the past. More to the point, in no part of Labour's empire were the values of the past still more potent and adored than in its party in Scotland, whose social and political mores were a matter of utter mystery even to members of the party in England.

V

The existence of utter mysteries such as these might also help explain why Labour, in carrying out the late Mr Smith's wishes about Scottish devolution, made two important and potentially devastating mistakes in particular. The first was that the party, led from London (and whose principal Scottish luminaries spent more time in Westminster than in their own homeland), sedulously fostered the belief that the Conservative party had become so hated in Scotland because it was a predominantly English party. This view was reached, it should not be forgotten, before the incontrovertible evidence of that party's winning no seats at all in May 1997: a result which poured an accelerant on this already incendiary conviction. Labour, with its great preponderance of Scotland's seventy-two MPs, complacently felt it had the perfect antidote to the loathed Conservatives. Labour appeared to be as much a Scottish (or for that matter Welsh) party as it was an English one. Indeed, in some regards it seemed more Scottish than English.

The Prime Minister had been educated in Edinburgh. In his first cabinet the Lord Chancellor, the Chancellor of the Exchequer, the Foreign Secretary (that is, three of the four great officers of state under the Prime Minister), the Defence Secretary and the Chief Secretary to the Treasury were all Scots. These ministers were among the most high-profile in the Government, so to the country as a whole the Government appeared to have a remarkably Scottish flavour. Two other cabinet ministers, including of course the Scottish Secretary himself, sat for Scottish seats. This meant that a third of the cabinet was Scottish, whereas only one-eighth of the parliamentary party came from Scotland: a great success for the Scots in terms of their participation in and influence over the Union, and (one would have thought) a clear return on their investment in it. Any properly opportunist Labour politician would have said to the Scots in 1997 that they had been rid of the Conservatives for at least fifteen years, and it might be better not to rush into anything (like devolution) that might precipitate separation from England and the gravy train. However, this ignores the regrettable reality that, in public at least, the great majority of Labour politicians from both sides of the border could not bring themselves to believe or acknowledge that the late Mr Smith's devolution plans could possibly lead to anything so unthinkable as separation.

However, despite the achievement for Scotland and the Scots of dominating the British government after May 1997, Labour's reward has been to decline in the opinion polls in that country. This is because they had not realised the truth about Scotland's feelings towards the Conservatives. That truth was that the

Conservatives were not, as a general rule, hated in Scotland because they were an English party. Nor, even, were they hated so much for the subsidiary, but significant, reason, that they were a party that under Mrs Thatcher believed in a capitalism blue in tooth and claw, when such a philosophy was anathema to the more instinctively socialist Scots. They were hated, above all, because they were the Government of England. It may well be that their status as the Government of England was highlighted by their commitment to so many things that were unsympathetic to the distinct political and social culture of the Scots, such as rabid capitalism and the reduction of the size of the state (though let us not forget that Adam Smith, who might best be credited with the invention of these economic concepts in their modern and dignified form, was Scottish). The SNP talks, in its 1998 policy document *Towards the Scottish Parliament*, of 'the common concerns of enterprise and compassion most Scots share'. That is code, of course, for saying that the English are selfish, greedy bastards (which many of them undoubtedly are, though it is hard to believe that such traits are entirely unknown in Scotland), whereas the Scots have a more developed sense of community and are happy to pay high taxes to support it. It may be that Labour thought that, by not being Thatcherite, it would avoid at the ballot box the type of obloquy that had been reserved by the Scots for the anti-compassionate since the coming of Mrs Thatcher.

However, it may equally be that, so Thatcherite is the New Labour economic policy, with its rigid and commendable belief in the monetary theory of inflation, that the Scots now have found again the very reason to punish a British government that they thought had departed with the Conservatives. Whether or not that is so, the Scots are certainly, their devolved parliament notwithstanding, reminded of one other incontrovertible fact: now Labour has become the Government of England – albeit one peopled, amusingly, by a legion of Scots. Therefore, they have inherited the opprobrium of a people who, it seems, have simply had enough of rule from London, whoever is dispensing it. The ICM survey for the *Scotsman* newspaper of June 1998 found that 77 per cent of those polled felt that SNP 'stood up for Scotland', whereas only 43 per cent felt the same about Labour.

It is hardly surprising that Labour, for all its overt and almost professional Scottishness, is so regarded by the Scots. The Scots, unlike too many of their counterparts in England, are not stupid. They are infinitely more political, and politically conscious. They are especially alert to one feature of the Blair cabinet. That is that there has been a stunning reluctance on the part of Labour ministers to abandon Westminster and to participate instead in the equally noble, and for them perhaps much more legitimate, cause of ruling their own homeland. The Scots themselves can draw only two conclusions from this: first, that these ministers regard Scotland as hardly worth the trouble when there is so much fun to be had in England – a bit of an insult to those committed to a devolved Scotland – and second, that the present devolved arrangements are something of a sham in the eyes of experienced politicians. No wonder that, contrary to the expectations of most in the Labour party, the Scots themselves do not regard devolution as the end of the matter, but as the beginning of the end of the matter.

Whereas Labour's first big mistake was rooted in their per-ceptions of their main rival party in England, their second has been rooted in perceptions of their own party. 'New Labour', which transformed the party's fortunes in England, is still largely irrelevant to Scotland. It had long been respectable for the middle classes to vote Labour in Scotland, something it did not become respectable for the middle classes in England to do until Mr Blair was invented, and which suggested that, at last, the political sophistication that the English ought so to envy in the Scots was at last coming into their bloodstream too. Apart from Labour's having already won the middle classes over in Scotland, and having won them over on a more traditional, socialist, redistributive programme than the middle classes in England would ever have swallowed, there is a culture more of behaviour and style than of ideology that separates Labour in Scotland from Labour in England.

As English (and many Scottish) Labour MPs will be the first to admit, there is still much to be done with the Scottish Labour party. A string of local government scandals has exposed important parts of the party machinery in Scotland as fundamentally corrupt, factionalised and anti-democratic. One MP, apparently persecuted beyond endurance by a rival faction, took his own life not long after the glorious election victory. His persecutors included, it was alleged, a brother MP, who found himself expelled from the party for gross misconduct in 1998. In a separate incident, another Scottish MP was suspended from the party soon after the election for electoral irregularities. Perhaps taking fright at all this, the central Labour party machine in England has sought to prevent those with what might be termed unacceptably left-wing credentials, such as the outspoken and uncompromising MP Dennis Canavan, from becoming Labour candidates for the 1999 Scottish elections – an imperialist interference that has given great heart and opportunity to the SNP. Many in the Scottish Labour party resent the treatment they are receiving from London, and from 'Uncle Toms' in their own ranks who have made their number with – indeed, have to all intents and purposes become – the English Labour establishment. Division and disunity have therefore broken out; and with the Conservative party a pathetic wreck, and a spirit of independence abroad, it is no wonder the Nationalists have capitalised so brilliantly upon the opportunity presented to them. It leads one to realise that among those in England who will have the greatest shock if Scotland becomes independent and England is left on its own, there will be a substantial number of supposedly sophisticated English Labour party activists, not all of them English by birth or descent.

There is, perhaps, something to be said for the notion that

Labour made matters worse by the nature of the franchise for the 1997 referendum. Some have argued that had expatriate Scots elsewhere in the kingdom – defined as those with a Scottish place of birth on their birth certificates – been given a postal vote in the referendum, the majority for change would have been far less than it was, and the nationalists therefore denied much of the comfort and impetus that the result in fact gave them. Given that some estimates claim that as many as five million Scots live in England, and a million English live in Scotland, it might be feared that the question of separation becomes messier than it might be: though the number of Irish who live in England, and the number of English who live in Ireland, would seem to suggest that that is a consideration almost unworthy of troubling ourselves with. The decision on Scottish independence must be taken by the majority of those living in Scotland, and accepted by those who live in England, however imperfect the electorate. The very fluidity of population movements in these islands is, of course, one of the great arguments for Unionism in the broadest sense and for a common nationality; but it should not be forgotten that it is not the English who have sought to break up these arrangements, either in the past with Ireland or in the future with Scotland.

For the moment, it is the Scots who hold the future of the United Kingdom in their control. To exist, the Union as a political entity needs the ancient nation and Kingdom of Scotland. If Scotland goes, then there is no such thing as a United Kingdom, even if the Welsh and the Six Counties are clinging on to their differing forms of association with the Crown. Wales's position especially becomes untenable. In such a circumstance, Wales could not seriously consider, for economic reasons, going the same way as Scotland. Nor would any but a few fantasists in the ranks of 'The Party of Wales' imagine that they could. Nor should the English, in the eventuality of Scotland's going, contemplate funding Wales's absurd assembly, which in its imminent incarnation and in its last conception under the Callaghan government has never seemed to be much more than something to keep the Welsh sweet while their fellow oppressed in Scotland were getting a new toy to play with.

If the Scots do decide to leave the Union then a new choice needs to be offered to, and made by, the Welsh. One alternative is full independence, with 'Wales independent in Europe' taking its chances with all the other countries on earth. The other, less extra-planetary version is support by the English taxpayer in return for government on an absolutely equal basis as any part of England might expect: in other words, how Wales always used to be governed, with the dropping of the pretence of which English politicians of all parties have long been guilty that Wales is somehow deserving of special treatment compared with any part of England. The tinpot assembly would go; the recently reformed local government in Wales can do what local government properly does; and the Welsh could send their forty MPs to Westminster, and have a say in influencing and running a country far richer, more significant and powerful than their own little principality could ever be on its own. If the English had the courage to put the choice in those terms to the Welsh – and it is an entirely fair and logical choice consistent with the democratic fundamentals applying elsewhere in Britain – then it is not difficult to predict what decision the Welsh, who have shown themselves to be intensely realistic during their two devolution referenda, would make.

VI

'If the English had the courage'. That is the point. So deeply imbued in the English is the idea that they owe the other peoples in these islands a living, in repayment for England's disgraceful history of conquest and oppression, that talking to the Welsh, or the Scots, in the plain-spoken, adult fashion that they as civilised, responsible human beings have the right to expect, is still utterly alien. Telling them that, in the modern world, hard choices (to use a phrase much beloved by the present Prime Minister) have to be made, and that in the true spirit of post-imperialism nations cannot be life-support systems for other nations (or for peoples who misguidedly think they are nations) is deemed to be unspeakably vulgar and tactless. Worse, it might provoke a hostile response. Therefore the English do not do it. They wallow, instead, in unreality. They construct the pretence, rampant at the moment, that all the devolution that is now taking place need have no impact on the Union, as they think they understand it, at all. Therefore everything can carry on as before, no confrontations need take place, and nothing will have changed. That is what being British, in the English estimation, generally means; and it is largely why Britain, mostly run by the rigour-free appeasement-addicted English, has declined continuously throughout the century.

According to the opinion polls, there is a strong risk that the English, by thinking of themselves largely as British, will before too long be thinking of themselves as an adjective that has no corresponding noun. The things the British English thought were part of their country – the Scots Guards, Balmoral Castle, John O'Groats, the Loch Ness Monster, Famous Grouse whisky and, when they do not confuse him for an American, possibly even Mr Sean Connery – will at a stroke become foreign. Apart from sharing a land border and, up to a point, a language, there need be nothing to distinguish England's relations with Scotland from England's relations with Finland, Greece, or any other small and insignificant country in the European Union. And the inhabitants of England will have to become used to thinking of themselves as English only.

There have been, it is true, encouraging signs in recent years that this process may be underway, but they are limited. For the purposes of many sports, as we have already noted, England

and Scotland have long been separate entities. It was at the time of the 1996 European soccer championships that, in order to make emblematic their support for their country, English fans resurrected the Cross of St George, for so long buried as a constituent part of the Union flag. To most people, this flag had only ever been seen flying from the towers of parish churches on royal birthdays and other such important events. It was a reminder that the Church of England made no pretence to be anything other than English, and as such had better advertise itself under an appropriately English badge. Or, we had seen it as children painted on the shields of toy knights in armour off on some imaginary crusade.

To those who do not allow their lives to revolve around soccer, the renascence of this flag was curious. It was like bringing a long-forgotten ornament out of a long-closed room. That flag has been somewhere in the collective memory; we all knew it was up in the attic somewhere, but we could not quite remember what it was for, or what its point was. This is hardly surprising; it had not done serious service since 1707, after which it was superseded by the first Union flag. The only sentimental or patriotic associations it could possibly have would be ones that had to be manufactured afresh. It has not, probably, been a coincidence that those who wish to parade under the St George's flag have suddenly become numerous at a time when England, through the British mass media, is being bombarded with anti-unionist sentiment from Scotland. Equally, there may be a perfectly rational explanation for the fact that the cross of St George is seen so often now as a sticker in the windows of London's taxi cabs.

It may all have much to do with the fact that a feeling is growing up that if the Scots wish to be shot of England, then the English should make no effort to argue against them, or to stop them. Instead, the English may be coming to a point where they are ready to assert their own separate and distinct identity: and a necessary preliminary to this re-awakening of national consciousness may be the re-adoption and flourishing of England's own emblems as symbols of their ability to be independent. However, the mentality behind this might also be defensive. There have been unfortunate elements in Scotland in recent years – and their activities have been reported in England – who have made it clear that they simply loathe the English, and do so largely on tribal grounds. A soliloquy by a drug-crazed character from the celebrated film *Trainspotting* was, without any visible irony, recycled by the student wing of the SNP in a leaflet – much to the embarrassment of the SNP leadership, who are trying to be sensible and statesmanlike in the run-up to their attempt at power. The observation ran: 'We are colonised by wankers. We can't even pick a decent culture to be colonised by. We are ruled by effete arseholes.' (There are many among the more enlightened English, paradoxically, who would not disagree with a word of that and who, indeed, would recognise those shortcomings as being among the main causes of their country's long-term degeneration.) For his part, Mr Andrew Neil has observed, with regret, that 'These days, if England played Iraq, you could count on a substantial and voluble minority of Scots to be backing Iraq.'

Matters get, it seems, more unpleasant than that. On 5 November 1998 the *Daily Telegraph* ran a report under the heading 'English children suffer race abuse at Scottish schools'. It was, admittedly, hardly a scientific survey that prompted the story, but it still raised causes for concern. A theatre company in Edinburgh organised a short story contest for children. Those entries from English children being educated in Scotland reflected experience of bullying and bigotry far worse, it was claimed, than suffered by Asian children in the same schools. The bullying reflected, also, the cultural divide that has grown up between England and Scotland, and how it appears to be rooted in politics. 'One English girl aged 13 complained that she was nicknamed "Thatcher" and another aged 16 was constantly referred to as a "stupid English bitch". Other youngsters were called "Tory bastards" and "Yuppies".' This seems to provide clear evidence of the unwillingness of the Scots to ally themselves with the economic revolution undertaken in England in the 1980s, whose basic monetarist principles are being followed by the present Labour government, and suggest envy and resentment at the economic good fortune England has enjoyed as a result of those policies.

Nor are children the only victims of this mentality. In July 1998 an English labourer, Mr Tony Bolton, said he was driven out of his job at a Scottish engineering firm by the racial abuse of his workmates. He was awarded compensation of £2,499 when his claim was accepted. Mr Graham Power, the deputy chief constable of Lothian and Borders police, claimed racial discrimination when not shortlisted for the job of chief constable of the Northern Constabulary, based in Inverness. He was awarded a settlement out of court. In England, happily, the English accept with relatively little distress the appointment of Scots not only to senior jobs in the public and private sectors, but indeed to the highest level of their government and, without turning so much as the proverbial hair, in numbers quite disproportionate to Scotland's place in the Union. Part of England's economic success has been due to the fact that, for all its reputation as a country built on racial and class prejudices, its managers now understand that jobs must be given to those who are best qualified to undertake them successfully, irrespective of whether that person happens to be Scottish, black or from a sink council estate. The siege mentality that elements in Scotland have created for themselves – for one searches hard for evidence of deliberately harsh or spiteful treatment by the English in recent memory – means that such enlightened attitudes are not always apparent north of the border.

The English identity, which is apparently (if not always flatteringly) obvious to outsiders, ought not to be so difficult for the English themselves to reconstruct. It undoubtedly predominated in the projection of 'Britishness' in the great imperialist age. Its associations with Jingoism and with the rampant cultural colonisation undertaken by the Victorians have contributed more than most things to the sense of embarrassment that still hangs around the idea of 'Englishness', whatever that elusive, subjective and indefinable quality is. In recent decades especially, not least under the pressure of political movements in Ulster, Scotland and Wales, it has seemed like good sense and good manners to play down Englishness. Those same soccer fans who have resurrected the Cross of St George have themselves been much to blame in this, since the most usual stereotype of modern-day English nationalism has been the fouling of foreign towns by English soccer hooligans, and the mindless beatings-up of harmless and often hospitable people whose main offence is not to be English.

The other countries in this, at present, United Kingdom seem to have a different means of expressing their identity. It is one that, fortunately, does not inevitably include the kicking of three-year-old French girls in cafés in Marseilles. For the Scots and increasingly the Welsh, like the Irish before them, their sense of identity is a crucial part of the means of the liberation they seek from the English yoke. It therefore attracts international sympathy even when it is expressed in forms so violent that they even exceed those used by English soccer hooligans – note, for example, the licence given to Irish Republican terrorist organisations by the Americans for many years, and by certain countries in Europe. Having once been so powerful, and ignoring the fact that they are now so weak and emasculated, the English are routinely seen as the villains of the piece. They get, in the eyes of many abroad, what is coming to them. It is the payment of various historical debts. The use of nationalism against the English is only to be expected; the use of nationalism by the English cannot but be feared, deprecated, and discouraged.

The strong sense of identity, both cultural and national, that the Irish, Scots and Welsh have developed has helped fuel the political movements of separatists in those countries. It has made them believe not just that they could face, but that they actively want a future apart from England. Now, the English must do the same, if they are to cope with the realities of a disunion that may be forced upon them. A certain amount of public relations work will be required; not least in the English's owning up to the world that they have at last shaken off their delusions of power. They have to understand, and then to make it clear to others that they understand, that the purpose of their nationalism is defensive, not aggressive. It is to preserve a culture and a way of life that is understood by and familiar to those who are, or consider themselves to be, English. These things are to be preserved in the context of a distinct state with a sovereign parliament For the benefit of the mischievous, the blinkered or the fearful, the English must stress that they do not seek to re-establish their own sense of nationalism for anything other than peaceful reasons. English national identity is not to be the foundation for a desire or need to oppress or conquer anybody else, nor is it to be based on exclusive criteria of race or religion, or upon racial or religious theories. The English need to say that they are looking for a nationalism that will allow them to be just like the other tribes in these islands: independent, coherent, and with a proper idea of who they are and what they, as a distinct part of civilisation, believe in. If it helps all sides to come to terms with these developments, there should be a general recognition that the English are doing this because the Scots, by gesturing that they may break the Union, effectively leave the English with no option but to reinvent themselves. The alternative, which we shall discuss in part three, is for England to cease to be a nation altogether, but instead to take its place in a Europe of the regions.

Once the English accept that finding an identity for them-selves is a positive and not a negative undertaking, they shall only be at the beginning of solving their problems. Those searching for an identity need to know what they are looking for. It is less easy for the English to define their identity than it is for the Scots or Welsh to settle theirs. Oppression, real or imagined, has its uses, and in this instance it has been useful in uniting people (who imagine they are oppressed) around certain cultural, historical and political totems. The English have their own totems too, but in many cases they are regarded as British. The other difficulty in making the English understand who they are is the fact that for decades schools have steered their pupils away from a detailed understanding of an English, as opposed to a British, heritage; and even British heritage has often of late been depicted as unsavoury, not least with reference to past imperialism. In this context, it is also often easier to remember that for a few years in the 1930s Stanley Baldwin, Neville Chamberlain and their cronies took the coward's way against Hitler than it is to recall that for six years their fellow Britons died in large numbers in a broadly successful attempt to atone for the politicians' mistakes.

Having for generations been too self-conscious to assert their national identity, and before that having come under intense cultural pressure to express that identity as British, it is hardly surprising the English do not know what it is. It is regrettable, but equally unsurprising, that young men of the same age as those who died on the Somme or in the North African desert most readily define their Englishness by going abroad and beating up foreigners who, unlike at earlier times, have no quarrel with the English. The English emphatically cannot allow themselves to develop a nationalism in which people are united by the shared joy they take in attacking, or even in simply disparaging, people of other nationalities. Yet what can even educated – let alone uneducated – English men and women today hope to know about an English identity, when there has not been a distinct one for the best part of three hundred years? And, indeed, given that England for the century before the Act of Union was ruled mostly by Scots and latterly by a Dutchman, was not the notion of an English nation run by the English already ancient history by 1707?

The answer, of course, is that the English identity – as instinctively felt, understood and expressed by the ordinary people of England – has never gone away. It is present, if latent or misdefined, in the consciousness of everybody who is English, whether by descent, birth or by the conscious act of self-identification as a resident. Everyone has his own personal view of what it constitutes, which is why attempts to define 'Englishness' are pretty fruitless, and why the phoney chocolate-box representations of the notion (Cotswold churches, Big Ben, Beefeaters and the rest) are best ignored. Englishness is an entirely metaphysical concept; it is a sense of allegiance and a sense of belonging, a sense among the English of knowing what is theirs. Each English person is free to choose the icons, sentiments and parts of history that make him or her feel English. If Scotland goes, and the English identity has to be manufactured afresh, it may, for many people, be simply a question of changing the name on the signpost in their mind. Instead of saying 'I am British, I think British thoughts and I do British things', they say 'I am English, I think English thoughts and I do English things.' It is what the Scots, the Welsh and the Irish do, and it has not proved too hard for them, or caused them much pain. All it means is the English realising that they are (to borrow an old Irish phrase) 'ourselves alone', and not any longer part of a conglomerate.

It is, or it should be, so simple as that. It is the finding again of the English identity by means of a straightforward act of subtraction. The English need to understand that the country to which they belong is what is left when and if the Scots choose to become a sovereign state: or what the SNP call 'Scotland independent in Europe' (we shall deal with that particularly ridiculous contradiction later). They would, were the Scots to go, belong to the country they had always belonged to; all that would have changed is that their country would no longer be part of the larger entity that was its external expression for three hundred years. The people who live there would not have changed as a result; their virility would not have been impugned; they would not have become weaker, less significant, and certainly not poorer. It would be, as the politicians are wont to say, a new dawn for England.

VII

Such a leap of the imagination, when and if Scotland has gone, is what the English must execute if they wish to flourish as a nation. It would constitute a basic acceptance of what would be the new reality. There is no point the English whining and moaning about the end of the Union. They need, instead, to summon up the intelligence to realise that if the Scots will it, there is nothing to be gained by standing in their way. Indeed, the English need to wish the Scots a fair wind, because they have nothing to gain from reinventing the ancient enmities with the country next door. There may well be, as we shall see later on, certain activities the English can undertake for their tiny neighbour on a commercial basis, to the benefit of both parties. This new relationship, which may well be foisted on the English whether they like it or not, can only be conducted satisfactorily if the English embark upon it in a clear-headed, unsentimental, unwistful way, which is why they need to have confidence in themselves. That can come only, in the first instance, from knowing who they are.

England's great history should be a help in this respect. It ought to provide many of the values and much of the inspiration that a civilised, peaceful and advanced nation needs to draw upon in rediscovering itself in a modern world. That is why it has been so wicked that recent generations have not been taught about English heroes, about English civilisation, about English achievements. The list – the core English values (which are not, of course, that different from the values of other peoples in these islands, but which it is essential for the English at the time of their independence to reassert to themselves and to others) – is impressive.

Fundamentally, the English are a Christian people, predominantly Protestant, though one (since, at any rate, the repeal of the Test and Corporation Acts) tolerant of other faiths and denominations. Their main festivals – Christmas, Easter, even in origin some of the bank holidays – are Christian. The English Crown, which gives continuity to the nation and has been a main source of its political stability, and freedom from revolution, is an overtly Christian institution. The monarch is the Supreme Governor of the established – Christian – church. The United Kingdom parliament at Westminster was originally the English parliament and its example has been followed around the world; England is the mother of parliaments. English law, always separate from Scottish law, is an enduring institution. England's ancient universities were at the forefront of establishing liberal democratic thought. England has its roll of heroes, of poets, of scientists, of painters, of thinkers, of composers, of architects, of reformers, even its own saints. The English must remember that these are their people, and that there is a continuous thread representing the English genius right down to our own century. The foundations on which the reinvention of England must take place are solid, and their effect benign.

Yet the English must not delude themselves into thinking that England is anything like it was in 1707, let alone in 1603, or 1485, or 1066, or at any of the other climacterics in history to which the English might want to refer back. The English state has constantly evolved and has been constantly re-formed by waves of immigration. That has been as true in this century as it was in the past, even if this century's immigrants have been more exotic in origin and more diverse in culture than those who came before them. There is always someone, at any juncture in England's history, who is assimilating – sometimes willingly, sometimes helplessly against his will – and somewhere the process of anglicisation is being carried out. Not the least impressive thing about England for the English to bear in mind is just how attractive their country has been, and remains, to those from elsewhere.

The English mix is already striking. A few Romans no doubt stayed behind with the Ancient Britons and Celts they had found in what is now England. Then (in no particular order) England has received Angles, Saxons, Jutes, Danes, Norsemen, Normans, Welshmen, Jews, Scots, Huguenots, Irish, Afro-Caribbeans, Indians, Pakistanis and Bangladeshis. At once it becomes clear that while there may undeniably be an English race of predominantly Germanic origins, the English citizenry cannot be racially defined. England as a nation is not a multiracial society in the way the race relations industry would like to pretend it is – over 90 per cent of people in England are white, Christian and of northern European ethnicity. It is a predominantly Anglo-Saxon, Norse and Celtic country with small but significant minorities resident here. For the moment, all are British subjects; 'English', correctly used, has hitherto been a vague label of ethnicity, not of citizenship. That will have to change if England gains its independence. The new English citizenry would be markedly different in certain important respects from what it was when Oliver Cromwell was the last Englishman to rule over an English state. It would, however, be mostly from the same stock, and it would live in the same acres: and those who have come from elsewhere would identify themselves not with Britain, but with England. However, to make this identification complete the English state – like any newly independent nation – would have to think seriously about the difference between a society that happily accommodates people from and gladly tolerates various cultures, and one that actively encourages multiculturalism.

It is a self-evident truth that if multiculturalism is actively encouraged, it must be at the expense of the indigenous culture in all its forms. At a time when a nation is re-establishing itself, that could be destabilising and harmful. Indeed, it is hard to see why minority cultures should be forced upon a majority at any time. That is not the same as disparaging or belittling other cultures: indeed, such an illiberal stance would contradict a great English ethos. One of the core values of an independent England must be the centuries-old tolerance and hospitality traditionally offered to settlers from abroad, particularly from those countries with whom Britain, as was, had imperial ties. Indeed, the greater economic strength that ought to flow from the sundering of England's ties with the more dependent parts of the present kingdom should make England even more of a land of opportunity. However, those who came to a newly independent England would need to accept that they were entering a country that was not settled in the world like dear old, somewhat unsure-of-itself, Britain, but which was passing through a period in which it had to reinvent itself as a separate entity.

This means saying clearly to those from other cultures that, not just in the privacy of their own homes and in their own communities, but anywhere in England, their own way of life and their own form of religious worship will be protected and preserved like all essential freedoms within the law. English law must, however, be their law: their children must speak English at school, and be taught about English institutions and English customs in just the same way as the ethnic majority is. At home and in their communities and places of worship, children from the minorities can of course speak their own languages, observe their own customs and celebrate their own history, but there can be no question of giving other cultures equal weight in the English school curriculum. It is vital, most of all for the sake of the happiness and security of the immigrants themselves, that the people the English welcome to England integrate with English life, and that English life is seen clearly to be something

43

sufficiently humane, tolerant and decent for them to be happy to integrate with it. Similarly, as we shall see in part three, the propagation and provision of culture to adults that involves the spending of public money must, in fairness, be weighted towards English culture, not solely to exhibit and perform the achievements of past generations of English, but to encourage the English cultural continuum into the next millennium. Of course, English culture can be supplemented and amended by external influences, as it always has been; but it cannot be replaced by them, or made an object of embarrassment.

There must be no need, and there must be seen to be no need, for those who are of other than English descent, but resident in England, to fear English nationalism and independence. The immigrant communities in Scotland set a fine example in this regard. There is a body called Scots Asians for Independence, which has over five hundred members, and who actively support the work of the SNP. There is no reason why Asians in England, or Afro-Caribbeans for that matter, should not be equally involved in support of English independence. Indeed, it must be true that by their working with political parties who eventually come alive to the benefits and realities of English nationalism, those of non-English descent will best ensure that their interests are taken care of in a new, independent England: and by making their voice heard in the independence movement, will ensure that however English the cultural base of the independent country might be, it will not have any trappings of racial exclusivity. English culture will continue to evolve, and evolution is preferable to engineering changes in the interests of tokenism. Only if the minorities join in the independence project with the majority will they be able to play their part in the evolving culture, and make their own enduring contribution to Englishness.

It is important not to discount history, and historical influences, too much. That waves of immigrants have assimilated so well is partly down to their, for the most part, adopting English

44

ways, and living by English laws and customs while observing their own within their own communities and families. That some immigrant communities have retained their own cultural diversity should not be a threat, provided that diversity does not embrace a determination to obliterate aspects of the English host culture, to defy English law or to violate legitimate English sensibilities. The exercise of the freedom of immigrant communities in a free country seldom puts them at odds with the status quo, though the slitting of sheep's throats in streets in the western suburbs of London has, quite understandably, caused disquiet among a Christian country of animal-lovers who prefer their lamb humanely slaughtered.

There are things that make England distinct from Scotland or Wales, and it is more than having your own soccer team. In their laws and customs, their interests and habits, their religious practices (or lack of them), their means of education and their ethos of enterprise, the English have much about them that marks them out both as different, and as being at the end of a continuous and continuing national experience.

The tolerance and pluralism that have always characterised the English way of life are vital to it; but they cannot, especially at a time when the country is rebuilding its separate identity for the first time in three hundred years, be exploited by advocates of multiculturalism to turn England into an amorphous non-state that contradicts its history and the cultural and social values of the vast majority of its population. Freedom and equality of opportunity are, in fact, by far the most effective weapons against the threat of multiculturalism that would, if allowed to take root, destroy the English nation once and for all by destroying its identity and challenging its widely accepted values. The *quid pro quo* for the English's absorption of diverse minorities into the new English state must be the willingness of those who choose to be part of that state to respect and tolerate English society and culture.

If any further reassurance is needed by the English about

the acceptability of their promoting their own culture – and, knowing the diffidence of the English, it almost certainly will be – then let us consider the view the Scottish Nationalist Party takes of such matters. In that party's own 1998 conference handbook, the importance of Scottish culture was explicitly stated. It made clear that the cultural renascence of the Scottish nation and the renascence of the nationalist movement went hand in hand, starting after the Great War. 'Just as Macdiarmid took Scots and Scottish literature out of the kailyard, so the SNP has sought to give to the people of Scotland the confidence and self-worth to allow them to move forward to independence', the handbook stated. If such sentiments are applicable to England and the English – and it must strongly be contended that they are – then the more so is the statement that follows it. 'The SNP has always realised both that Scottish culture needs political autonomy and that independence can only grow out of a self-confident culture.' The SNP plans to do this by heavily promoting the Scots and Gaelic languages, and their literature, in schools. It plans to train teachers accordingly, and says, commendably, that it is 'not afraid to advocate radical change. This is in contrast to the recent practice of the Scottish Office, who smothered the publication of a recent paper on Scottish culture in the schools'. That last point is indeed a matter for regret, but one has heard anecdotal evidence for years of the same thing happening to English culture in English schools. Only thirty years ago, for example, children in English schools learned old English folksongs and sang them with gusto: now, irrespective of whether or not they have children from ethnic minorities in their class, they are more likely to learn to sing African National Congress protest songs, and to study the religions of far-flung parts of the Orient.

The SNP adds that Scotland's new parliament 'should be a place which is not afraid to see Scotland grow culturally and to show that the cultural tradition which gave rise to the SNP will be one of the forces which carries Scotland forward to independence'. In another SNP document – *Delivering the Best: a draft Local Government manifesto* – this message is hammered home further. Quite rightly, the manifesto says that 'Gaelic and Scots will be protected and nurtured'. Also, 'SNP councils will ensure that Scottish history and Scottish content of the curriculum is seriously addressed by the Government.' It is noted too that 'we must also cherish our culture and its appeal to tourists, so that we retain a strong sense of identity and a confident face to the rest of the world'. In *Towards the Scottish Parliament*, the party proclaims that 'it is through our books and films and plays and music that the strength of Scottish culture past and present is made accessible to all. We must embrace education and culture as one, and provide the services to educate, enlighten and entertain for the benefit of all'. Later on, the same document says that 'our culture gives us a sense of pride and destiny, and helps define us on the global stage ... the Arts should be incorporated throughout the state education system so that the seeds of cultural curiosity and creativity are planted young'.

All this is laudable and understandable; what is more, an Englishman can laud it and understand it all the better as soon as he realises that the same must be true for England, and of the forces that carry England forward to independence. It may well be true that the British Scots did their bit of eliminating Scottish aspects from the teaching of the history and culture of Scotland, to make it seem a more uniformly British place. It may even be that, reflecting the inevitable weight of England in the British experience, there ended up being more English history taught in Scotland than might be tasteful to those of a nationalist bent. That, though, was for a different nation: if the Scots are once more making their own nation, they will inevitably have different requirements. It is equally inevitable, as in all *soi-disant* liberation movements, that the Scots should view the failure to propagate their history and culture in Scotland as part of the deliberate brainwashing and propagandising

47

that the conqueror undertakes among the conquered, especially when the conquered's history and culture has some sophistication and appeal. It is why the Normans rebuilt the perfectly charming churches of the Anglo-Saxons after they invaded England in 1066, and why Hitler had highly intelligent books written by Jews burnt in public.

The English must think about this. There are important keys here to the re-establishment of their own distinct identity, and they should not be afraid to use them. Unless a conscious educational and cultural effort be made to promote the English culture and heritage, the effects of England's unsought independence from Scotland could be unpleasant. It will be difficult for the English, though in part three suggestions will be made as to how best it can be done. The English regard many of the trappings of civilisation as effete, boring, and the province of only the highest social classes (whereas, ironically, the highest social classes all too often lack the brain required to appreciate and interpret these trappings even remotely properly). There remains a strong instinct among the poorly educated to express national identity by violence and force, and not by recourse to the benign achievements of earlier generations of English. It is the culture of boorishness and unsavoury nationalism that will take root, unaided, in the event of English independence, which is why some urgent educational direction must take place to prevent it. What would the English rather their independence movement drew its nourishment from: men with haircuts like lavatory brushes, who fashion a recreation out of kicking foreigners, and whose definition of being English is reliant upon savagery, alcohol abuse and physical strength; or from Shakespeare, Milton, Dickens, Elgar, Constable, Montgomery and Churchill?

VIII

Defensive, constructive nationalism has been an important part of the re-establishment of those new or reborn nations in eastern Europe in the last ten years. These are nations whose identities as sovereign states have been visible for the first time in over half a century following their absorption by the Soviet empire. These countries have practised nationalism without, so far, lapsing into extremism; most have adopted western liberal ways and have put themselves at the table of the western family of nations. It is their understanding of who they are, of how they are nations, that has allowed them to flourish after years of oppression, and which should help guarantee their freedom in the future. They show a positive cohesion, a sense of common, peaceful goals, and the only battles they wish to fight are for market shares and economic prosperity. What has happened in the former Yugoslavia exemplifies a struggle between defensive and aggressive nationalism; and displays how nationalism can be a liberator and not, inevitably, an oppressor.

What England needs to strive for – and it should not be difficult, given the settled and democratic traditions of the country – is such a nationalism; one that protects its own, rather than seeks to engage in belligerent conduct against others. Such a departure on the part of the English should be utterly acceptable to everyone else, with the possible exception of those in England and on the continent of Europe who wish nothing more than to build, for the moment by stealth, a European superstate.

Many Scots would argue that what is here being counselled for the English is exactly what they seek to do for themselves, and they would be right. If the Scots feel oppressed, if they feel they wish to make their own way in the world – having heard, but rejected, the arguments in favour of Union – then they should not be prevented from doing so. They are likely to make a better fist of surviving in that new order by having a coherent, sensible national identity, as are the English. It is ironic and odd that the decision to have an English nation again is likely, in the end, to be taken by the people of another country. That it should be left to the Scots not to decide upon just their own independence, but on that of the far more populous and wealthy nation to which they are attached by union, is typical of some of the less commendable side-effects of the English character: notably diffidence and disinterest in political developments. However, just because the independence of England may well come upon it by accident, that is no reason not to exploit it, and turn it to the advantage of England and its inhabitants. Above all, the English must realise that the loss of Scotland is not the end of the world – at least, not for England.

The English genius, whether of the mercantile sort popularised by the Tudors, or of the more politically conscious sort in the century before the Act of Union, did not disappear in 1707. Nor was its incorporation into the British mentality something that should have altered or diluted it, any more than certain Scottish characteristics and peculiarities have been lost after that country's three hundred years of Union. The English had a distinct social and political culture before a United Kingdom was invented. It will be there again, if only by default, should the United Kingdom be disinvented. What the English must draw strength from is the contribution their country and their forebears have made to Britain during the three hundred or so years that that political entity has existed.

The main contribution is obvious: people. Of the 58 millions in these islands, 50 million are English by residence. There are, of course, many Scots, Welsh and Irish (not to mention people of more exotic descent) living in England, as was often the case also before any Acts of Union. Large centres of population mean economic activity; and what has attracted so many from the other parts of the kingdom (and, indeed, the world) to England is the wealth in which they can share here. That brings us on to England's second great contribution to the kingdom:

money. The English have subsidised the Scots and the Welsh for centuries. There is no question but that the English taxpayer would benefit immensely from Scotland's going its own way. The latest figures suggest that the best part of £8 billion more is put into Scotland by the Treasury each year than Scotland raises in revenue. That equates to a cut in income tax of nearly four pence in the pound at the basic rate for the English.

People from all over the kingdom fought and died in wars for Britain, though sight of the Scottish national war memorial at Edinburgh Castle reminds any Englishman that there was a time when the idea of the common cause within the Union was given a tragically concrete expression. As Dr Niall Ferguson has recently recorded in his book *The Pity of War*, no fewer than 557,618 Scots enlisted in the Great War, and 26.4 per cent of them lost their lives – a death rate exceeded only by the Turkish and Serbian armies who, as Dr Ferguson also notes, lost a higher proportion of their men to disease. England made its own massive contribution of blood, as every village war memorial painfully records. In other respects, though, it must be admitted that the English have fallen short in what they have done in the name of Britain. All too often, the English have been content to be passive partners in the enterprise, averse to risk, lacking the desire for innovation, short on inventiveness.

The Scots, for example, took a commanding role in building the Empire, leaving it to the less muscular English to administer it and to find most of the finance. Canada and New Zealand especially would barely have existed without the Scots; the existence of the churches of obscure Scottish religious sects in certain African countries, such as Malawi, testifies to the crusading zeal of past generations from Scotland, and also exemplifies the greater importance of religious life to the Scots compared with the English. In many ways, the fact that the British Empire no longer exists makes inevitable the retreat of Scotland from the Union, because the Empire was for a couple of centuries Scotland's main commercial and social benefit from that arrangement. Now, there is no such shared project on which the Scots and the English can embark with such fervour and commitment, and with so implicitly fine an understanding of the right division of labour.

Because the Scots took education seriously long before the English ever did, the Scottish intellectual legacy is immense, whether manifested in inventors or thinkers. As Mr Andrew Neil has also said: 'For a small, cold, mostly barren country on the periphery of north-west Europe we seemed to have made a disproportionate contribution to the intellectual and economic progress of mankind.' In Scotland as long ago as the beginning of the nineteenth century, even peasants like Carlyle's parents made the sacrifices to send their children to school and university. In England, hardly any children of working-class origins could aspire to a university education until after 1944, such people (irrespective of their merit) being seen as factory fodder ever since the Industrial Revolution. Among the English upper classes, for whom university was more easily attainable, it was not regarded as within that class's spirit of Corinthianism to excel too much intellectually. The seeds of Britain's decline were propagated in England, not least by English liberals of the twentieth century – so different from their shrewd and ruthless predecessors from the Victorian age – whose guilt complexes and underdeveloped thought processes brought a welfare state and numerous other forms of crippling self-indulgence.

It is perhaps largely because of these shortcomings that the English might be wary about going it alone now, even though they may have no choice in the matter; but such fears ought immediately to be discounted by the contribution England has made to the kingdom during the post-imperial period. London's position as an international financial centre has much to do with the prosperity of the whole country, but particularly with the whole of South-eastern England, within the arc from Southampton to Peterborough via Oxford. There is some cause for optimism for the future in England. In recent years, educational standards have been taken more seriously, which ought eventually to lead to a better educated, more able population. A cult of home ownership has helped improve the housing stock, and with it the sense of responsibility of much of the population. Many of the most hideous blights on the English landscape, the workers' barracks ordered by Harold Macmillan in a towering act of cynicism as Housing Minister in the early 1950s, are either falling down or being pulled down. The lesson has been learned that if a society puts its people in sties, they live like pigs. All that stands between England and a proper sense of self-respect is a reform of state welfare that finally relieves a small but poisonous proportion of the population of the notion that self-reliance is an evil.

If such schemes and policies to improve the lives and chances of the English people are set in train, and at the very time when England is setting out afresh in the world again, one of the distinct attitudes of the old English will be nurtured: that the state is fundamentally a bad thing, and that the greatest happiness English people can have is to be left alone. Fortunately, the cash injection that England could enjoy if it were relieved of the burden of supporting Scotland would allow independence to be embarked upon with every possible resource and, as Sir Edward Elgar once put it, 'massive hope in the future'.

IX

We are almost ready to start upon England's reinvention, having shown that England has the self-confidence to be a nation again. However, one danger about all this still prevails. It is that, because of England's rich history – because it is, despite the absurd and self-serving claims of some politicians to the contrary, an old country – those who make the leap of seeing themselves as English instead of British take a romantic, and not the necessary practical, view of what that means. Too many of those who have identified themselves as English resort to the sort of sentimental terms so beloved of Stanley Baldwin, when he addressed the Royal Society of St George in 1924: 'The sounds of England, the tinkle of the hammer on the anvil in the country smithy, the corncrake on a dewy morning, the sound of the scythe against the whetstone, and the sight of a plough team coming over the brow of a hill.' That might have been the case in 1924, though only just. If one updates the imagery – 'the hum of the petrol pumps at the filling-station, the sound of the Radio One breakfast programme emanating from the window of an "executive home", the clouds of dust thrown up by the combine harvester and the sight of a tractor coming over the hill' – some of the lustre wears off. Baldwin was, perhaps, more accurate in his estimate of the general characteristics of the English people, made in the same speech: '... we are less open to the intellectual sense than the Latin races, yet though that may be a fact, there is no nation on earth that has had the same knack of producing geniuses ... we grumble, and we always have grumbled, but we never worry ... The Englishman is made for a time of crisis, and for a time of emergency ... when he once starts he is persistent to the death, and he is ruthless in action ... there is in England a profound sympathy for the under-dog. There is a brotherly and a neighbourly feeling which we see to a remarkable extent through all classes. There is a way of facing misfortunes with a cheerful face ... Then, in no nation more than the English is there a diversified individuality. We are a people of individuals, and a people of character'.

Yes, you will say, all very true. Many of these characteristics are, we instinctively feel, still visible today. But are they? And if they are, how far are they really English characteristics, as opposed to British ones? We may just have to accept that if we start to think of certain things as English, we shall see they are Scottish too, with differences only at the margins. Old fears will creep up on us: why on earth, some of the English will say, should we be passive while Scotland makes moves towards independence, given that we two peoples have so much in common, and that God has plainly ordained that we should not be put asunder? Such notions need to be rationalised. Ideally, given all the similarities between us, Scotland would not be sundered from England. However, if it chooses to go, the English people can react in two ways: they can make an international exhibition of themselves by screaming and shouting about something that they are powerless to stop, or they can calmly accept it. Such a sundering may be bad for Scotland: but, as has been stressed before, that is a problem for the Scots, not the English.

Separate from Scotland, England would be a more urban country than Britain is. In England, especially within a hundred miles of London, even the countryside has the knack of seeming relatively metropolitan. It would be marginally more ethnically diverse than Britain, having a higher concentration of people of Asian and Afro-Caribbean descent. It would be more affluent than Britain: and that brings us on to the real differences that exist between the temper of the English and the temper of the Scots.

Scotland has been more wedded to the articles of welfarism than, in general, England has. The culture of enterprise, similarly, has lately been more apparent in England than in Scotland. Demographically, there is more of the 'new middle class' – the very people who voted Labour in 1997 – in England than there are in Scotland. The traditional community structures, and indeed the sense of community, are more visible in Scotland than in England, and there is, as we have noted, a greater sense of the influence and presence of religion. The religious fundamentalism to be found in parts of Scotland tends to be found in England only among Moslem communities: such commitment seems to be regarded by the English as deeply un-English, as is proved by the ultra-progressive and, at times, apparently non-religious nature of the Church of England.

It would simply be the case, after separation from Scotland, that the English would carry on being just as they are. They would not need a sentimentalised or romanticised vision of themselves to give them heart for their future existence without the Union, however much that might comfort some of them. That England has produced Chaucer, Shakespeare, Milton, Wordsworth, Dickens, Purcell, Elgar, Wren, Hawksmoor, Nelson and Kitchener will be of precious little concern or relevance to most of those who will have to form the new England, though it is always helpful to have such people around to enlist for inspiration. Despite its reference back to its heroes England will, paradoxically, need to stop living in the past – an essentially British past. The British legacy will, of course, be of great benefit to England. There is no question of international isolation occurring as a result of independence. Those continental or global organisations in which Britain has played a part will be there for England, and England, an entity reduced only marginally from the days of Britain, will be as important to those councils as Britain was. It may not – probably will not – be the same for Scotland, but that is a calculation the Scots have to make for themselves. For England, the calculation is made for them by events, but it is still hardly a painful one. Only once it and the English people see that this is so, and that it is possible to have a decent future as an independent nation, can that future be embarked upon with confident hope of success, prosperity and peace. Letting Scotland leave the Union, if it wishes to go, would not be the ultimate act of constitutional defeatism: it would be, on any number of levels, one of the rare smart moves the English have ever had made for them.

TWO

An English Comedy

The weight of evidence about England's economic power, and of that country's absolute lack of dependence upon Scotland, seems to be less adequately appreciated than it should be. Even the most sceptical of the British English ought to accept that, in the event of Scotland's choosing to become independent, the English state that would be left would be more than capable of flourishing. It would be healthy for the English to begin to foster this entirely reasonable attitude. Should Scotland choose to go it would, indeed, be of great tactical and emotional benefit to the English to have prepared themselves, and made themselves confident, for the new adventure upon which they would have to embark. In reality, there would be little difference between England on the day before Scottish independence and England on the day after it. No new strategic or economic peril would have struck. Instead, indeed, the English ought to be planning how best to spend their new-found wealth, and deciding what image of themselves they wish to develop and project to the world.

However, it is almost comical that so many in England instinctively persist in the notion that the English nation would in some way be inadequate alone, and that happiness for the English people can be achieved only by their country's membership of a larger political and economic unit embracing as much of the geographical entity of Great Britain as possible:

which, for the moment, is the United Kingdom. This belief has long been, also, one of the motors driving the move towards regionalism, and the incorporation of English regions with other European ones in some sort of superstate, which we shall consider in the third and last section of this tract. The argument such people advance runs more or less as follows: that as there is a growing desire for separatism within the United Kingdom, and as England must inevitably be a pretty poor show on its own afterwards, then it – like Scotland and, for all we know, Wales – could have the privilege of being 'England Independent in Europe'. In other words, England would be diminished to the point where it was simply playing the role of a culturally distinct region – or, more likely, group of regions – within the great European superstate. Most of the really important decisions – on the economy, foreign policy, possibly even defence – would be taken for it by a central bureaucracy in Brussels, or by other institutions such as those regulating economic and monetary union. The details behind this assumption are never made clear. They certainly have no foundation in economic logic. If England, with 50 million people, is too small to be viable, then many of the countries of modern-day Europe ought to have no right to exist. What seems to drive this belief – indeed, some believers make no secret of their motivation – is a fear of nationalism. They have seen too many men with shaven heads and steel-capped boots waving St George's flag.

For others, however, whose lack of belief in England is borne of good old-fashioned defeatism, it is the prospect of regionalism that compels them to argue for the maintenance of the Union even at this late hour. It also compels them not to admit the logical contradictions of a Union being carried on despite devolution and the fuel devolution is supplying to the separatist movements. This quite traditional self-blinding to reality is touching in its consistency, but it further entrenches the air of unpreparedness for what may be about to happen to the English. The more taken by surprise the English are, the less they will be able to reconcile themselves quickly to their new nation and its new status. Therefore, the more vulnerable will they be to the assaults of the regionalists, who have a vested interest in never allowing the English the time or the opportunity to discover whether or not their lives can go on not just as normal, but in a mode of prosperity and contentment superior to that known before.

The reluctance of the English to believe that they can be happy without being in a United Kingdom is, of course, also part of their incipient fear of asserting themselves, still bearing as they do a form of post-imperial guilt at their largely imagined role as the oppressor of the Scots and the Welsh. This oppression has little basis in fact. The Scots volunteered to join the Union in 1707 largely because of the economic desolation of their own country, and the huge amounts of Scottish funds that had been lost in an ill-fated attempt to plant a Scottish colony in Central America. The Welsh are so convinced about their not being oppressed that only 25 per cent or so of them could be bothered to support the forthcoming devolved assembly when they were offered the choice in September 1997.

A much more considerable objection to English nationalism is the natural concern the English feel for their brothers and sisters in these islands, and the doubts they harbour about the possibility of Scotland's flourishing after independence. It would certainly be hard to reconcile with the English experience the fact of having a foreign country on the same island as England. However, as has been pointed out, there may well be nothing the English can do to prevent it. As for the consequences for the Scots that, I repeat, must a problem for them to resolve, and for them alone. There is an old adage about people who make their beds subsequently lying upon them. It applies very much to the Scots in the decisions they must make in May 1999 about the colour of their new assembly, and any subsequent choice – should the SNP form an administration – about whether or not to pursue full independence. The English will just have to learn to let Scotland go if that is what Scotland wants to do. Many of an older generation remember the decades of poverty and isolation into which the twenty-six counties of Ireland subsided after partition, a new isolation and a poverty even less relieved than when the country was supported by Britain. Any English who fear for Scotland, and who specifically fear that it might turn into a wilderness, need not just remember that this would be Scotland's own choice: they should also note the likely financial help that would be forthcoming to Scotland, at least to start with, from the European Union, and also the export markets to which Scotland has established access. Such benefits were not available to the Irish for fifty years after partition, and the Irish genius has always been more cerebral and less practical than the Scots'.

It is certainly true that some things would be strategically easier for the British peoples if one government alone controlled these islands: but, since the establishment of the Irish Free State, that has not been the case, and now Scotland is to have its own opportunity to fragment the state still further. There can be no doubt that the strategic unit of the British Isles is, from England's point of view, best under the sway of what are currently the British armed forces. It was troublesome in the extreme, during the Second World War, to have Ireland neutral, and Irish ports unavailable for use by the Royal Navy in its attempts to defend these islands – though that was a self-inflicted wound by the British, since Neville Chamberlain had handed back to Eire the Treaty Ports as part of his general appeasement policy in 1938. It would have been better, during the war that followed, for the United Kingdom not to have had to deal with a Prime Minister such as de Valera, who felt it expedient to shame his country for a generation upon Hitler's death by visiting the German Embassy in Dublin and signing the book of condolence for that deceased genocidal maniac. However, despite such inconveniences and provocations, Britain still managed to be on the winning side, and Himmler did not have an opportunity to open a concentration camp on the Curragh to deal with those in Ireland deemed to be racially inferior or politically troublesome.

The fact of England's sharing a land border with Scotland, and therefore theoretically being susceptible to an invasion from the north should a third party overrun the weakened defences of an independent Scotland, is scarcely worth considering. Even in the remote possibility of a conventional land war being waged in which England was involved, and in which English territory was under threat, the idea of a hostile power launching the invasion from a starting point four hundred miles north of the capital, having first taken the trouble to conquer Scotland, is absurd. As for the Navy's role, its control of the seas around these islands would be unaffected by Scottish independence, just as it was before 1707 and, indeed, just as it managed to be without the cooperation of the Irish in 1939–45. These are, in any case, the most pessimistic constructions that can be put on what would happen to our defences after Scottish independence, for they assume some sort of uncooperative stand-off between the two countries, or Scotland choosing to be defenceless. Neither of these situations, we must fervently hope, is likely to happen.

There are thousands of Scots under arms in the British Army, and in the other two fighting services. Their allegiance is to the Crown. Strategic matters are one respect in which the existence of Crown, after independence, could be helpful. Indeed, the Crown might be the only quasi-political and non-geographical entity that might, after Scottish independence, legitimately be prefixed by the adjective 'British'. In an opinion poll on the future of the monarchy in Scotland taken in September 1998, 61 per cent of those asked said they would want the Queen of England to be Queen of Scotland also – which has some sort of historic logic to it. This followed a commitment by the leader of the Scottish Nationalist Party to have that party argue for the retention of the monarchy in any independence campaign.

Scotland would in such a circumstance be like Australia, New Zealand or Canada in this respect, with the Queen as head of a state separate from England. Although this policy has caused some controversy among the SNP, which has more than its share of determined republicans, a Scottish republic is for the moment not an inevitable or even a likely product of Scottish independence. Should an independent Scotland become a republic that, too, should be of no more concern to the English than it is when some African despotism, or South Sea island, chooses to replace our shared head of state with one of its own.

After Scottish independence the Queen would have her army in Scotland as well as in England. It would not, of course, be so simple as that. It would not be the case that the only difficulties in the re-ordering of what is now the British Army were likely to be administrative. Someone has to pay for these armed forces, and it is not clear that the Scots would be able to manage their share without a severe strain on their Treasury. If maintaining an army was a problem, a navy or an air force for Scotland might be extremely economically ambitious. It would be for the Scottish government to decide what forces it could maintain, or whether it would be better advised to try to sustain some sort of defence pact with the English. This would probably not be a defence pact of the sort nations are used to making, where each has its armed forces that act in concert with each other. It might more likely mean the maintenance of a Scottish army, with most other defence requirements bought in from the English on contract terms.

Assuming the SNP adheres to its present, admittedly some-what controversial, policy on the monarchy, the Crown would continue to be the ultimate authority in Scotland even after independence. It is just that the Queen would have a separate Prime Minister there who would have the responsibility to give her advice not just on such parochial affairs as have been parcelled out to Scotland under devolution, but on matters of high policy too, such as defence and foreign affairs. It can be safely assumed that one of the first activities in the formalising of the relations between the two newly independent states of Scotland and England would be such a permanent defence pact as described above. This would be built upon the fact that the armed forces of the two countries would still have their shared loyalty to the Crown. Defence policy could be co-ordinated between England and Scotland at a ministerial and official level just as it has long been in NATO between Britain and other nations. If it turned out that it was practically and economically more sensible for Scotland to be provided with much of its defence by England, that could be done on a commercial basis, the advantageous terms of which would recognise the historic and enduring importance to England of military cooperation with the Scots.

This is bound to be a sensitive matter with the SNP, which might regard such close inter-relationships as making Scotland effectively a client state of England's, and removing an important feature of its independence. Scotland may have little choice in the matter; defence is one of the policies upon which rampant unreality creeps into the SNP's calculations. However, if it wishes to be independent, in this most important area of all it must take the consequences. Either Scotland can go largely unprotected, thus discounting an ancient, noble and glorious military tradition and making itself vulnerable even in today's supposedly safe world, or it can allow the English to help out. There is also the economic question of what Scotland would do with all those pugnacious young men from Glasgow who currently earn gainful employment in the British armed forces and who, if they do not directly serve Scotland, would find themselves serving instead in what might well come to be termed the English Foreign Legion, or as tartan Gurkhas.

The SNP is not, in fact, quite so hostile to post-independence cooperation with England as some of those on the party's wilder shores have made out. The party has long claimed that it would like the two countries, as well as Wales, Scotland

and both parts of Ireland, to be members of an 'Association of British States', whose existence acknowledged the new realities of the independent status of the former parts of the United Kingdom. The idea is also calculated to attract wavering union-ists to the SNP by making them feel that the map is not being completely torn up. It also, as the SNP's leader pointed out in a speech in Ireland in the summer of 1998, bears a close resemblance to the idea of a British–Irish Council that came out of the Northern Ireland peace process. If such an association is to have any use other than as a talking shop, or as a non-legislating federal parliament, it could be as the superintending authority for the permanent defence pact between England and Scotland: as well as providing a forum in which the two sides could discuss, without any obligation or much formality, any matters of foreign policy that might affect relations between two such close neighbours.

It may also be that England has a certain reliance in matters of defence upon the Scots. The SNP is felt to be generally opposed to a nuclear policy: it certainly looks forward to the decommissioning of nuclear power stations. Its attitude to nuclear weapons is for the moment unclear, and is enabled to remain so not just by the removal of the threat at the end of the Cold War but by the general, and not inevitably correct, view that the SNP cannot possibly ever be elected. England, however, could still need some of Scotland's deep water facilities for its nuclear submarines: although some military opinion believes these submarines are unnecessary since Russia appar-ently ceased to be a threat, or would only be deployed in far away theatres of conflict, and that they could in any case be berthed at Devonport. If Scotland has no anti-nuclear policy of its own – and, given England's nuclear arsenal, it might be futile for it to mount an opposition to the nuclear deterrent – then it should be happy to earn the foreign exchange that would flow from leasing its deep water ports, and any other facilities of which the English had need, to its neighbour. This would offset some of the cost of Scotland's own defence requirements, and salve the conscience of the British English about providing for their former dependent relative. In any event, the realities that are likely to develop after independence will almost certainly ensure that England does not need to have any strategic worries about the break-up of the Union, because Scotland will be well defended – not least, probably, by the English.

II

If the English can reassure themselves that a future remains for Scotland's relations with the Crown, that not all ties of sentiment have to be sundered, that the regiments alongside which their grandfathers served in the last war will still be on 'our' side, that the Queen can still live at Balmoral when she chooses and pop down to the Braemar Gathering when she is bored with her house guests, then that may help them realise that the loss of Scotland does not portend some sort of British cultural apocalypse. It would be an important part in the necessary learning process, that one does not need to own or control one's neighbours in order to be on good terms with them, and to share the same island contentedly. Such are the cultural and temperamental similarities between England and Scotland – between the English and the Scots – that the happy coexistence of two neighbours on a similar wavelength ought almost to be taken for granted. Indeed, given that so much discontent in the relationship today seems to derive from Scottish resentment at the supposed colonisation of their country by the English, and increasingly from English resentment at having to support the Scottish dependent relative, then things might be more cheerful all round if independence occurred.

Having considered the strategic question of the defence of the realm, the next issue that will have to be addressed, before the English admit that they are happy for them and the Scots to go their separate ways, will be one of filthy lucre. This, however, is relatively straightforward. The economic arguments are, so far as the English are concerned, hugely in favour of English independence. The great claim of the Scottish Nationalists for the last quarter-century is that the North Sea is full of 'their oil'. This is an interesting and, so far, untested assertion. Fundamentally, the question of Scotland's oil will have to be settled under international maritime law. The Scots are not immediately helped by the fact that, in judging what would be their territorial waters off the east coast, the land border with England runs south-west to north-east. It therefore carries on north-east across the North Sea to the international limit. It therefore puts quite a lot more of the North Sea under English jurisdiction than the Scots might like, and certainly much more than under the Scots' assumption that the line goes due east across the North Sea.

As one exceptionally enlightened Scot, Mr Bill Jamieson, pointed out in his excellent 1998 Centre for Policy Studies pamphlet *The Bogus State of Brigadoon*, the SNP's claim that 90 per cent of North Sea revenues belong to the Scots is simply 'rhetorical'. The case that could have to be fought under international treaty law between England and Scotland would not help relations between the two countries, and would be likely to end in a substantial disappointment for the Scots. So, too, given the unpredictability of the level of oil revenues, would the amount of money the Scots could hope to raise from what oil ends up being theirs. Current returns are dismal. Also, the British jurisdiction over the North Sea is still based, as much as anything, on the ultimate control of those waters by the Royal Navy. As has already been suggested, Scotland is likely only to have the services of a proper navy to call upon if it enters into a defence pact with the English.

When it comes to dividing up the oil quite a lot, too, would depend on whether the Shetland Islands decided to consider themselves Scottish. There is no reason why they should. For

594 years the islands were a dependency of Norway's; they have been under the Scottish, and then the British, Crown for the 530 years since. At a time when Scotland is reinterpreting its relationship with England, there is every cause for the Shetlands, by the same token, to reinterpret their relationship with Scotland. The Scots would be wise to take the view towards the Shetlanders that the English ought to take towards the Scots: that if they don't want to stay in the family, then there is no point trying to coerce them. They might feel better off becoming a dependency of England's, since England needs their revenue far less than Scotland does, and is more likely to have public money to reinvest in the islands. England is also likely to maintain a lower rate tax regime than the Scots would. This last point is one many businesses in Scotland are already aware of, which is why some of them have issued threats to move to England should independence occur. Scotland, on the other hand, would see that much of the Shetlands' wealth (at whatever rate it was taxed) was spent in Scotland, for the benefit of millions of people who have no connection with the Shetlands whatsoever, and for whom the Shetlanders feel no particular affection. The Shetlands might even become like the Isle of Man, and set themselves up as a tax haven, specialising in offshore companies and generating huge amounts of foreign exchange in the process. Or, they might choose to ally themselves with Norway, given their greater proximity to that country. If the Shetlands' territorial waters do not, for whatever reason, end up providing Edinburgh with black gold, then the SNP's economic fantasies, already pretty preposterous, will enter into the absurd.

For the English, on the contrary, the road to Scottish independence is paved with gold. Were they to be an entirely cynical people, motivated only by harsh materialism, the English would, indeed, do everything to encourage separatism and separation. When the Scottish people realise the high price they have paid for setting themselves up as the Greece of the north –

principally in the form of massive taxation – it will be the English who stand to benefit. Nor will this benefit reveal itself merely in the simple fact of lower taxes for English citizens. England will be the location of choice for many businesses who do not intend to be penally taxed, but would rather benefit from Mr Gordon Brown's generous corporation tax regime in Britain. The SNP has a draft policy of cutting corporation tax in an independent Scotland, but its Treasury minister would need to see the books before embarking upon it. Any cuts would need to be paid for by raising taxes elsewhere, but the SNP claims to have a plan for this. However, its policy of abolishing the ceiling on National Insurance contributions – one such money-raising wheeze – could well leave Scotland without much of a senior executive workforce, as it would effectively raise the top rate of tax at a stroke to 50 per cent. Those whose jobs give them a high level of mobility in their careers – especially high earners – would need little encouragement to be off. Such a taxation regime would hit middle managers hard also, given that lower earners would suddenly find a high marginal rate of taxation being imposed upon them. The Treasury has calculated that 250,000 Scottish employees, or 10 per cent of the country's workforce, would be affected by the lifting of the NIC ceiling – and these are, of course, the most successful 10 per cent in Scotland.

Nor would that impost necessarily be the end of the tax rises an independent Scotland would need to inflict upon its people. A deficit of about £8 billion a year would need to be made up once England's subsidy stopped coming to Edinburgh. So either taxes would rise steeply for almost everybody, or spending would have to be cut severely. As we have seen in other advanced economies in crisis, both strictures might be necessary: the EU is hardly likely to be able to find regular sums large enough to neutralise the pain, whatever some nationalists might hope. Not wanting to underplay this issue, Donald Dewar, the Scottish Secretary and Labour's candidate for First Minister once the parliament is established, warned his fellow Scots in his speech to the Labour party conference at Blackpool in October 1998 that voting SNP could create a £15 billion 'black hole' in the Scottish economy in the shape of a cumulative structural deficit by the end of the first four-year parliamentary term – equivalent to 20 pence on the basic rate of taxation for Scottish taxpayers, or nearly doubling the existing basic rate. This calculation accepted the SNP's figure of an average £3.75 billion deficit per year over that term, which itself is wildly optimistic compared with recent out-turns. Trying to fund even the most optimistic deficit would lead either to higher taxes, or higher interest rates because of increased borrowing, or most likely both.

As a result of this tough taxation regime, the north of England could well enjoy a boom not seen since the Industrial Revolution, as the front line of Scottish enterprise moves just across the border, onto the new industrial estates that would inevitably spring up in Northumberland, County Durham and Cumberland. With businesses would come people: well-educated and successful Scots people, skilled workers in the new industries, people with earning potential able to make a handsome contribution to the communities in which they settle, managers, innovators and entrepreneurs. Thanks to Scotland and England both being members of the European Union, there would be no such thing as border controls on the immigration of Scots nationals, no problems with movements of capital or personnel. This could hit Scotland hard, while benefiting England, not least in one often unappreciated way. Mr Jamieson has pointed out that Scotland now ranks among the top twenty financial and fund management centres on the planet. These operations are not registered charities. The slightest whiff of their being made subject to a harsher tax or regulatory regime, and therefore limiting the returns they can obtain on their clients' investments – not to mention the dividends they can pay to their own shareholders – and they will go elsewhere. That sort of business matters far more to Scotland than oil, with its declining price, can ever do, now or in the future.

The British government will permit personal taxation in Scotland to be varied from the national standard rate by only 3 per cent once the devolved parliament is in place. The rate could, of course, be set at whatever level the government of an independent Scotland chose. Allowing, potentially, a high-tax regime like this would be a further incentive to the professional middle classes to head south, to a land where they would experience no language barrier, little real cultural difference, a better climate and where, with increasing ease and frequency, they would be able to enjoy the company of their fellow Scots. This may all sound far fetched, but anybody who thinks that is so should consider the lessons of Ireland. It is only in recent years, since Ireland (after twenty years of membership) finally began to receive a level of bribery from Brussels that made their own independence financially worthwhile, that there have been sufficient incentives for well-educated and enterprising Irish people to stay at home. In the 1980s there was the famous episode of the press advertisement for the undoubted benefits of Ireland, which included a graduation photograph of a high-achieving class from Trinity College, Dublin. It was unhelpfully pointed out that only one of the twenty or so graduates in the picture was still resident in Ireland (at, I think I am right in saying, a seminary for the priesthood), while the rest had fled to London or New York to seek their fortunes, and escape what could only be described as a brutal taxation regime. Even now, the Irish top rate of 46 per cent is applied when income reaches a derisory £13,000 a year.

For decades before then, the aspirant Irish had headed either to America or England, not least to avoid paying crippling levels of tax on even modest incomes. There is no reason to suppose that Scotland's fate, in the short to medium term, is likely to be much different. Indeed, with gallant little Scotland just one of about a dozen countries likely to want to join the

EU in the next decade or so – Poland, Hungary, the Baltic States and so on – the Scots would be lucky indeed if the SNP's fantasy of a gravy train calling regularly at Edinburgh Waverley were ever put on the timetable. However that, of course, is yet another calculation that the Scots themselves must make.

Leaving aside the magnetic pull of England for Scottish businesses and skills, and the massive economies of scale that allow England to keep taxes down while paying for the panoply of nationhood, but which a population one-tenth the size will have a devil of a job affording, we then come to the most obvious benefit for the English of all. That is that every English taxpayer and every English business will be better off if England no longer has to subsidise Scotland. Despite the resurgence in Scottish enterprise thanks, paradoxically, to the economic reforms of their hated Margaret Thatcher, Scotland still receives far more than its fair share of the United Kingdom spending cake. In the 1950s it was estimated that Scotland had 12 per cent of the spend while contributing 10 per cent of the revenue. By the late 1960s per capita spending in Scotland was 20 per cent above the average for Britain as a whole. Nor did Mrs Thatcher properly earn her bad reputation: under her administration and that of her lamentable successor there were attempts to treat the massive unpopularity of the Conservatives both in Scotland and in Wales by the frequent spraying around of more public money. It failed.

In 1994–5, for example, during the last term of the last Conservative government, £30.3 billion of British taxpayers' money was spent in Scotland. In the same year £23.8 billion was raised there. The £6.5 billion subsidy would have been enough to take three pence off the basic rate of income tax, and thereby provide a great stimulus to enterprise, investment and efficiency. That dividend is still there, waiting to be claimed. It will also interest the SNP to know – as if they do not already – that of the £23.8 billion raised in Scotland that year, just £1.7 billion came from the oil on which their independent state is supposedly to be floated. By November 1997, the Scottish Office was claiming that the subsidy by England had risen to £7.4 billion in 1995–6, excluding the now derisory level of North Sea oil and privatisation proceeds. The Labour party's own figures suggest that Scotland accounts for 10.1 per cent of British expenditure, while raising just 8.8 per cent of British revenue. And, if the English were to be really businesslike about their acceptance of Scottish independence, they might like to start computing what Scotland's share of the British national debt would be, so that they could draw up an invoice for England to present to their neighbours on independence day.

In fact, the 1998 Public Expenditure Statistical Analysis threw up some interesting figures on just how well the Scots do out of the Union. In 1996–7 total expenditure per head of the population on services in Scotland compared with England was 24 per cent higher. In the previous four years, under the wicked Conservative government that the Scots were so happy to be rid of, it had been never less than 23 per cent higher and in two years 25 per cent higher. A closer analysis of the figures suggests just how badly the government of an independent Scotland would struggle to make up the difference. Spending on health and personal social services is 22 per cent higher in Scotland. On education it is 31 per cent higher. On transport it is also 31 per cent higher. On trade, industry, energy and employment it is 55 per cent higher. On housing it is 87 per cent higher. On agriculture it is a whopping 123 per cent higher. The absence of economies of scale for an independent Scotland, and the need to create new bureaucracies, inevitably mean that the Scots would have to spend far more than is presently the case just to deliver the same level of service.

With their customary good manners and almost comic reticence, the English might be expected to shudder at the notion of their making a profit – and a handsome one at that – out of Scottish independence. This is nonsense: just as many in

England utter the nonsense that it would be wrong to experiment with private management teams running parts of a National Health Service that managers in the state sector have proved incompetent to manage, because it would mean the firms concerned making money – God forbid – out of health care. Those who complain in these terms forget that doctors, nurses, ancillary staff and administrators all earn a living from health care; that drugs companies and equipment manufacturers and suppliers make huge profits from it; that building contractors are awarded fat contracts to refurbish its facilities, and so on. There is nothing wrong with making money. We all live off the profits of others, and will continue to do so until such times as Britain becomes a communist society, bound for complete economic ruin. If the English can make a four pence in the pound tax cut out of Scotland's deciding to become independent, that is a cause for rejoicing rather than shame. Subsidy is one of the great economic evils. It compounds inefficiency and the squandering of precious resources. Its elimination is always to be applauded. Let us just hope that, should the end of this particular subsidy come about, the English have the wit to spend their money wisely, in the productive sectors of the economy in the interests of prosperity and not, as the Scots have done, in the unproductive sectors in the interests of the pursuit of unreality.

III

The principal arguments advanced against Scottish independence are not, however, those of the defence of the realm or the optimum functioning of the economy, but of sentiment, national virility and *amour propre*. We are back to the predominantly English obsession with what other people think of 'us', pandering to that familiar insecurity. It is the obsession the English have that makes them feel that any further diminution

in the size of the national codpiece will make them an irre-
deemable laughing stock. The English, blessed as they also are
with a rough grasp of historical fact, imagine they have always
been part of – well, to tell the truth, the most important part
of – a United Kingdom. They like to console themselves with
the thought that Scotland, in particular, only saw a take-off in
its prosperity when it went into a union with England, and
when there was, later in the eighteenth century, the great joint
project of Empire on which to embark. However, what really
matters to many English people about the Union – the few that
actually ever think about it, of course – is that it is an organisation in which the English are (or are supposed to be) in
charge. In fact, it is just about the only one left of any significance of which such an assertion can legitimately be made,
despite a third of the Cabinet being Scottish. If the Union goes,
these people fear, then so too does that last reservoir of national
testosterone. Without being in charge of this particular club,
the English, some fear, would be nothing. There is also, it must
be admitted, that element in England that enjoys patronising
and subsidising the Scots, that loves paternalism, and which
fondly imagines that, somewhere, there are grateful Scots
doffing their Glengarries and tugging their forelocks in def-
erence to the kind English landlord. Evidence that national
defence will not be impaired, that prosperity for England can
only increase, and therefore that international influence
(measured, these days, not so much by battleships as by the
current account) ought not to wane is dismissed as wishful
thinking. There are atavistic, and therefore irrational, forces at
work here, and they must, in the English national interest, be
countered.

In these fears there are strong, and all too recent, echoes of
the disquiet and unease that accompanied the end of Empire.
The memoirs of those in adulthood in the period from 1945 to
1970 are full of the record of the trauma grown men felt at
seeing more and more parts of the globe no longer being

coloured red. The Commonwealth was invented as a preposterous placebo to soothe these psychological illnesses. It quickly, in fact, became the mother of all mechanisms through which the English could express and atone for their paralytic post-imperial guilt, usually by opening the national cheque book and sending the Queen or senior members of her family out to socialise with tyrants and murderers. With every surrender of territory, the reluctance among the old imperialists to lose what was left became more and more fierce. However, they soon were forced to realise that if these people wanted to go, there was nothing that could be done to prevent them. Some may even have become enlightened enough to realise how much better off Britain was without these responsibilities. Empire was only viable where the colonised wished to remain colonials, which is why it gave so many people such genuine happiness to be able to smash the living daylights out of the Argentinians in 1982, when they occupied the Falkland Islands. However, by the time of General Galtieri's ill-judged adventure, the British imperialist class was reconciled to its fate – which added an edge of almost sinful nostalgia to the Falklands exercise.

The last great battle over empire – or, to be more accurate, over its trappings – had, however, been fought out in the late 1960s, and concerned the British presence East of Suez. There were three uncontestable facts about this presence. The first was that Britain, whose economy had been spectacularly mismanaged by governments of both parties since the war, could no longer afford the luxury of far-flung military bases. The second was that with the surrender of the Empire in India and the Far East there were no longer British subjects, British territory or British supply routes that needed to be protected. (Indeed, a fat lot of good it had done the British in the Far East to have had such cover when the Japanese turned ugly in 1942.) The third, and most important, fact was that the public simply would not wear such a final, irrefutable act of imperial self-negation as was entailed in removing this unnecessary and unaffordable presence.

By the 1970s this largely sentimental baggage left over from Britain's imperial days had gone. Economic realities had left no choice in the matter. The pain had, though, been horrific, especially to backward-looking imperialists in the Conservative party, and among many of that party's adherents in the country. Such people regarded the contraction of British military power as akin to treachery. The fact that the trappings of this supposed power were mere pretensions in an era when Britain was in steep economic decline, relative to its competitors and especially to the most enduring superpower, America, seemed to strike almost nobody. The old imperial cast of mind did not, however, go away: it simply retrenched, within the moated splendour of the island of Great Britain, and awaited the next assault.

That assault may be about to arrive, in the form of a Scottish decision to pursue independence. It will be met by a last, and (if it is in the face of democratic will) largely pointless, roar of the British lion; a last desperate attempt to rekindle the fires of Unionism. Affection for the English among the Scots, and for the idea of a Union, is itself in such decline that if some form of Union does survive in its new, dilute, post-devolution form it will be for cynical economic reasons that benefit only the Scots. Since this would be likely to provoke resentment among the English it might not, as I have suggested above, survive indefinitely. It would be well for the English to remember the misery they caused themselves by clinging on to the vestiges of Empire in the 1960s, and to learn from that lesson. They must be made to see that the usual and often compelling arguments they advance for the Union's being a good thing – some of them practical, some of them sentimental – cease to be relevant immediately a majority of the Scots refuse to accept them. Remembering the problems caused by parliament's refusal in 1886 and 1893 to pass either of Gladstone's Home Rule Bills, and recognising the impossibility and pointlessness of coercing

Scotland to stay in the Union against its will, the English should clearly seek to maximise the benefits of Scotland's choosing to be rid of them. If the sense of identity discussed in part one has been created, or even if it has only just begun to be created, this process would be far less unpleasant than might otherwise be the case, for it could be embarked upon with hope, or even with excitement.

IV

In Scotland, the drive for independence is motivated by the people themselves. The SNP only exists, and is only now so strong, because an increasing number of Scots are prepared to support its fundamental aim. Nor can independence itself occur until such time as a majority of the Scottish people formally signify that they wish it to occur. In England, the procedure is somewhat different. This is as a result of England's being the passive partner in this act of constitution-breaking. Even when and if the breaking starts to take place, it is unlikely to be, first and foremost, a matter for the English people as to what happens next. The matter will be left in the hands of parliament to decide, and for individual political parties, whether government or opposition, to form a view. Any attempt to persuade Scotland not to end the Union will be led, under our political system, by the established political forces in parliament. Unless the matter is made a principal question at a general election, the English people are unlikely to be asked properly whether they wish their rulers to take the necessary measures to secure the Union – measures which might include a substantial increase in the level of bribes and other inducements paid by the English taxpayer to benefit the Scots. It is hard to see what further measures of self-rule, in addition to those already allowed by devolution, could be offered to the Scots without ending the Union *de facto*; any price they demand for staying in it is likely to be a financial one.

The overriding consideration for the political classes in England consequent upon a final push to Scottish independence will be what this means for them. An ethic of public service in our politics has long since passed down the sewerage system. There are, of course, even today some politicians left who are in it for what they can do for the country: just as it is still possible, when driving around England at weekends, even now to see the plume of steam coming from an old locomotive on a preserved railway. As a general rule, politics has now become a career. It is practised by politicians to the exclusion, or near-exclusion, of anything else in their lives. As a result of this regrettable fact, politicians are more often than not on the make: usually to satisfy their own egos and lust for power, fame and publicity, but sometimes seeing politics as a useful medium in which to attract women (or, as is now increasingly fashion-able, men) or to make money. The incidence of such behaviour is too well known, and has been so widely reported, as to require no elaboration here, however harmlessly and unintentionally entertaining certain reminders might be. However, because politics has now become for most MPs a full-time career with various regular and irregular perquisites, and because so few of them today know what it is to have the plush velvet cushion of the private income or independent means, it is only to be expected that they will want to think very carefully about what the break-up of the Union means for them before willingly accepting it.

The constitutional import of Scottish independence – which is, of course, grave – does not apply here: the question of how England ought best to reinvent its constitutional arrangements, should the Scots make that necessary, is addressed in the third and last part of this tract. What will really matter, and be of the most pressing concern, to the average modern Member of Parliament is what this means for the career, and prospects, of the average modern Member of Parliament. Anybody who thinks self-interest will not be brought to bear on this vital question has simply not been watching the conduct of British politics in the last thirty years or so, where MPs have routinely voted for all sorts of nationally damaging measures in order to retain the approval of the whips and the prospect of reselection.

It will be the political class that shapes the future (or lack of it) of the United Kingdom. The only legislation that might be necessary would be the repeal of the 1707 Act of Union; but first of all the political class might make the Herculean effort to see that it does not come to that, until such times as it is forced into it by the Scottish people. It may be that even a repeal is not necessary, a unilateral abrogation of those arrangements by the Scots being quite sufficient and humiliating enough. Should the Union end, then England ought to be able just to carry on, but the political class, or some of them, might have their own ideas, about regionalism and the like.

During this whole process – and be in no doubt about this – the private concerns of the political class will not be easily subordinated to the public interest. It would be argued that the stature of an English MP or English government minister would be unable to match that of a British one. It might further be argued that regionalism and the fragmentation of England itself would be the inevitable consequence of the end of the Union. Not only would MPs be less important: power would shift away from them, they would have less of a job to do, they would be less well-paid; there would need to be fewer of them. The fear would grow that, if this constitutional apocalypse were allowed to happen, the continuing ability of professional politicians to appease their wives, feed their children, pamper their mistresses or pay their rent-boys could, in some cases, be at stake. All too many of these people, as was shown among ex-Conservative MPs after the slaughter of the 1997 general election, are virtually unemployable in any other sphere. The basest fear of those outside the political class – the taxpayers –

must be that if the English political party machines decide it is in the best interests of English politicians for the Union to be maintained, then mechanisms (probably financial) will be found to make it more attractive for the Scots to stay in what, after devolution, will pass for their Union with England.

There are ample recent precedents for this: £6 billion was, for example, found by Brussels as a sweetener for the Irish to sign up to the Maastricht Treaty. If English MPs are told by their whips that additional bribes would make a difference, and if they are further told that their careers will almost certainly be limited in scope if so important a policy is not implemented, then English MPs may be relied upon to vote for it. Scottish and Welsh MPs would, understandably, be several times more susceptible to these arguments than even their English counterparts. It is entertaining to imagine the panic among that group of talented and ambitious Scots working their way up in the Labour party when they realise that their place in parliament, and in national politics, could be about to be snatched from them. Using a little more English money to guarantee the high-level political careers of a small number of Scots is likely to cause little concern to that small number of Scots; it is likely to cause even less concern to the massed parliamentary ranks of the Labour party, who know that by keeping a large number of Scottish MPs in the House of Commons they are helping to keep their party's grip on power.

Ireland, the Scots should note, has been left in an interesting position after accepting Brussels' largesse. The paradox of the relationship Ireland now has with the EU – that, having struggled for centuries to be rid of the English colonial yoke, the Irish now find themselves colonised by Brussels on behalf of a Franco-German axis – ought not to be lost on the Scots. It would be, as with everything else to do with choosing independence, a calculation for them, but the choice they are likely to face is between becoming a better-bribed client of England's, or a fully bought-up client of the EU's. The realities of that

choice are things to which too many in the SNP remain oblivious, otherwise, they would not insult themselves and their own
intelligence by talk of 'Scotland Independent in Europe'. Such
is the loathing of the English that many of these people feel,
however, that being bribed by Brussels is automatically a better
option than staying in bed with the English. It could be a
legacy of Scotland's ancient love affair with France, or what Mr
d'Ancona has perceptively called 'the sense of shared intellectual superiority spawned by the Scottish part in the European
Enlightenment'.

It is hard to see how any Scottish nationalist worth his salt can
even contemplate such a deplorable prospect for his country. All
the bogus phrase about 'independence in Europe' really means
is that Scotland will be abandoning its supposed dominance by
the English for a genuine dominance by a group of ruthless
European bureaucrats. The reasons for certain Scots nationalist
politicians fantasising in these terms are partly those of pique –
a few in Scotland really do hate the English with an intem-
perance that would have them on a racial hatred charge if the
targets were black or Asian – but also financial. The amounts
of cash being offered by the European Union, or so some in
the SNP think, are likely to match those the hard-pressed
English taxpayer is prepared to come up with. This is important
for the SNP because (as we have seen) for all their claims
that they could survive financially after independence, they are
talking nonsense. Scottish economic viability without someone
pumping in hefty subsidies from some wealthier part of the
planet or other is as real as the Loch Ness Monster.

It is, of course, none of an Englishman's business to try to
influence the touching and increasingly intimate relationship
that Scotland chooses to have with its new mistress in Brussels;
but there is no charge for advice. In any case, since Britain is so
large a net contributor to the budget of the EU, and since after
Scottish independence English taxpayers' money would still,
albeit by another route, be used to bribe the Scots, the English

have some right to point out one or two likely truths about this prospective special relationship. The greatest favour the English can perform for the Scots is to try to expose to them the lunacies of 'Scotland Independent in Europe' (though the absurdity is so self-evident that one might think that the Scots, even those steeped most deeply in anti-English delusions, could see it for themselves). The whole notion is what we used in the nursery to call cutting off one's nose to spite one's face.

In a press release of 7 April 1998 Mr Salmond, the leader of the SNP, announced that 'remote control of the Scottish economy from London has been and is damaging. At present, Scotland is suffering from high interest rates and a high pound because of the threat of economic overheating in the south of England. Yet the available indicators illustrate that the Scottish economy is far from overheating'. Mr Salmond's analysis is worth studying. Interest rates were high at the time when he spoke because too much money was about in the domestic British economy. This was largely because of the legacy of the cynical economic mismanagement by the last Conservative government. In its increasingly desperate bid to be re-elected, that Government allowed interest rates to remain lower than they should have been, and for the money supply to grow for more than two years at over twice the rate of inflation plus growth. It is certainly true that much of the overheating that resulted was seen in the most prosperous parts of Great Britain, notably in the south-east of England. The corrective action that had eventually to be taken by a refreshingly monetarist Labour government did not just temper appetites in what the advertising men call 'Roseland' – the Home Counties; it also, naturally, made it more expensive for Scottish entrepreneurs to borrow money, and for Scottish householders to find the disposable income to pay their mortgages. That meant less money going into the tills in Scottish high streets, and greater austerity all round. Equally, Scottish businesses have found it harder to sell goods for export because of a strong British currency abroad. That argument, however, must carry less weight, since exchange rates at time of writing are below what they were when Britain entered the ERM in October 1990, and way below what they were twenty years ago. Like most of British business (and this is a serious English disease), Scottish exporters seek continual devaluation as a remedy for their own poor productivity, inability to innovate and failure to find new markets for their goods overseas.

In a nation with a single economy, there will always be areas that suffer when an attempt is made to correct an excessive supply of money. During the great squeeze of 1989–92, and particularly during the Major government's disastrous experiment with rigging the exchange rate through the European Exchange Rate Mechanism, Scotland got off quite lightly. The real casualties were to be found in England, among the main beneficiaries of the Lawson boom that Scotland, and the North of England, had watched with mounting envy. By 1991, England was awash with negative equity. In some high streets, one shop in three was suddenly boarded up. Repossessions, bankruptcies and unemployment rocketed; Roseland was especially hard hit. The Scots, who had not risen so high in the 1980s, could now give full vent to their *Schadenfreude*. It is not always the apparently less prosperous parts of the kingdom that suffer during such times.

The charge Mr Salmond made about Scotland's suffering under the economic policies of his fellow Scot Mr Gordon Brown could equally have been advanced by, say, a representative of the people of Cornwall, though the people there would not, unless taking atavism to an extreme, have been able to introduce Mr Salmond's element of latent Anglophobia into their strictures. On a larger canvas, it was noted how during the oil price slump of the early 1980s the state of Texas could have done with an economy separate from that of the rest of the United States, but had instead to endure further stringency at an already depressed time because of the 'overheating' of other parts of the American economy.

Now just, for a moment, pause and think where all this leaves us in the context of the notion of 'Scotland Independent in Europe'. There will be supporters of the SNP who imagine that once the hated and contemptible English Treasury has finished having its evil way with Scotland, the Scottish economy can then be run by the Scots for the Scots. They should think again. There is, it seems, no great enthusiasm by the SNP to run its own currency. It does not conceal its enthusiasm for membership of a single European currency: it seems to hope, indeed, that the decision will have been taken for it, with the United Kingdom perhaps having already chosen to enter by the time a referendum on Scottish independence takes place. If such a decision has not been taken, the Scots would need to choose between alternatives: of running their own currency, fully convertible not just with the Euro but with the pound sterling, or of seeking to enter the European monetary union themselves. Realistically, if they choose the second option – as they claim they still wish to do – they would need to follow the first to start with, and prove to the European monetary authorities that they could run an appropriately tight ship. How they would manage to do that in the light of some of their other economic ideas would be interesting to behold. Labour claimed in November 1998 that the SNP would need to cut £1 billion of public spending if it were to meet the borrowing guidelines set for applicants to the single currency. Of course, the goalposts designed under the Maastricht Treaty could always be moved for Scotland, just as they have been and are being for other countries in the prospective economic and monetary union, but until and unless that happens we must assume Mr Dewar is right.

Let us just suppose, for the moment, that Scotland by one means or another finds itself having as its currency the European single currency – the logical conclusion of the ideology of

'Scotland Independent in Europe'. What does Mr Salmond expect would happen then? Can there be a guarantee that, instead of Scotland flexing the muscles of its independence 'in Europe', the country will sooner or later have to suffer a high interest rate regime because of economic overheating in the Rhineland, or Calabria, or even (indignity of indignities) the South-east of England? Of course not. Would the present species of latent xenophobia then be replaced by another, more diverse kind? Perhaps. Should this worry the English? Certainly not. Scotland needs to be afforded the respect due to all mature, democratic polities, and that includes being allowed to make its own hideous mistakes, and to have its own delusions. The fact of the matter is that a small state like an independent Scotland must either be properly independent, with all that entails economically, or resign itself to being part of a larger economic unit, whether Great Britain or Europe. Either way, its people may often find themselves disadvantaged because of what is going on in the vast part of the economic area that is not comprised of themselves.

No doubt the SNP believes that, freed of England's imperialist shackles, the Scots would have an economic miracle that would keep them in pace with the strongest of European economies. This, though, would take some doing. The SNP admits that 58 per cent of Scotland's trade is done with the EU. It does not own up to the fact that a gargantuan proportion of that trade is done with England (this is a problem the Irish have had before them). According to figures published in the Scottish Economic Bulletin of September 1998, 'the balances of exports and imports between Scotland and the rest of the UK and Scotland and the rest of the world are both negative (by an estimated £13 billion and £1.5 billion respectively)'. Just look at that first figure, and think what it means for Scotland's economic dependence on England. The English should whoop with delight at any prospect of Scotland's entering a single currency without England's having first made the mistake of doing so. If the Euro turns out to be so strong a currency as it has been trailed to be – and that is what its adherents, in Britain and abroad, believe it will turn out to be – then Scottish goods could, in many cases, be priced out of English markets, whereas English goods would be relatively cheap in Scotland, and the market for them there could only grow. Ireland, in planning to be part of the first wave of entry to the single currency, has taken a gamble similar to Scotland's, because of the great pre-ponderance of trade done with the UK by that country. The Scots, and the English, will need to watch very carefully what happens in Ireland in the months after entry. Of course, if the Euro turns out not to be a strong currency – if, indeed, the internal economic tensions of the Euro zone lead to its being a currency that is actually speculated against – then the prospects for Scotland would be severe. Not the least of these would be that English goods, on which the Scots rely, would be so expens-ive that great damage would result to Scottish standards of living.

V

We shall have to wait and see whether the most pessimistic interpretation is right, and whether English MPs would be prepared to bribe Scotland if that was what it would take to persuade the Scots to stay in the Union. Yet there is always a chance that the self-interest of English MPs might not, in this matter, be quite so easily dictated by the whips. Ironically, it would be likely to be MPs in what is regarded as the most unionist of the main parties – the Conservative party – who might have the greatest worries about such a scheme, even in the interests of maintaining their beloved Union. Many of them would instinctively object to the greater public spending involved, and to the failure of accountability it would entail. Many were embarrassed enough by the bribes paid to Scotland

and to Wales by the last Conservative government in the shape of special regional funds; they would not want to take that example any further, especially in the light on the lack of return on those earlier investments. Above all, they would not like to have to explain to their electors why they have been so free with their money, not least in directing it towards a group of people who profess less and less love for the English. Given the interest of the press in these matters now, the subsidisation of Scotland and the resentment it has the potential to cause are sure to become exceptions to the English's lack of political consciousness. However, whether the most unionist party of all would at last have the gumption to recognise the inevitable, and give up the ghost on Unionism, would require a leap of the imagination that is, for the moment, not quite in prospect.

As should be obvious from the great differences in their relative representations in England and Scotland, the main English political parties would in any case be affected by Scottish independence in different ways. Labour, having blithely considered that devolution would merely be a means of their establishing new power bases for their party in Scotland and Wales, instead has spent much of the last year secretly fearing that it may be trumped by the nationalists. The opinion poll ratings of Labour and the SNP have suggested a close call is likely at May 1999's elections: Labour may yet be saved by having adopted a system of proportional representation for the Scottish poll, which should deny the SNP a majority. If the SNP were to emerge as the largest single party, however, they could well run a minority government, albeit with some difficulty. With mistrust growing between the Liberal Democrats (who are likely to be the third party) and Labour over the British government's ambivalence towards electoral reform for the Westminster parliament, there can be no guarantees of the Liberal Democrats shoring up a Labour puppet administration in Edinburgh, despite the supposed cooperation that now exists between the two parties on various areas of policy.

According to its showing at the 1997 general election, Labour would lose fifty-six MPs at Westminster should Scotland become independent. Such a loss would also substantially reduce Labour's chances of forming the government in England. It would also rob the party of many of its most senior and, allegedly, able political practitioners. These men themselves would not be happy to face the alternatives either of finding seats in England, at a time when there might be a certain reluctance to entertain Scottish carpetbaggers, or of putting their considerable talents as statesmen to work on the Scottish stage, itself somewhat less grand than the platforms to which they have been used. Should these things happen, Labour could at least have the consolation of knowing that it had been the author of its own misfortune; yet that realisation is unlikely to make its pain any easier to bear. What it will mean is that, whether or not some form of proportional representation were introduced for general elections, matters are likely to be evened up in England compared with the result of the poll in 1997.

The 1997 result in England, which gave Labour the rare achievement of a majority in that country alone, was something of a freak. Labour is unpleasantly aware of this, and it explains some of the party's hostility to separatism. The Conservatives did unusually abominably for various reasons. Fundamentally, they were considered to be insufficiently Conservative – insufficiently principled – by many of their natural supporters. They had a recent history of division and weak leadership. Their senior practitioners were deeply unpopular with the electorate; worse, some had become figures of fun. The party had acquired a reputation for venality, sexual and financial aberration, incompetence and dishonesty. It was not that an unusual number of people voted Labour: it was that so few could bring themselves to vote Conservative. Although some studies have shown that there were substantial direct crossovers of former Conservative supporters voting Labour, the slump in the turnout compared with the 1992 election – down from 76.5 per cent to 71.6 per cent – suggested there was a high level of abstentions, presumably of Conservative supporters who would not vote for their 'own' party but could not commit the ultimate treachery of voting Labour. There was also the best part of a million voters, again presumably Conservative, who voted either for the Referendum Party or the UK Independence Party, on the grounds of the Conservatives being insufficiently sceptical about the benefits of the single European currency, or in many cases because of that party's complete failure to admit the issue of constitutional principle that was, and is, at stake in this matter. All these factors allowed the Labour party, on a share of the vote only slightly larger than won the Conservatives 336 seats in 1992, to win 418 seats in 1997.

However hard they try (and it is not entirely clear that the party has thoroughly mended its ways), the Conservatives look little better now, two years after that disaster, than they did when going down to defeat. However, part of the reason why Labour has been so rigidly disciplined since its victory, attracting accusations of control freakery, has been its incipient belief that the Conservatives simply cannot win so few seats next time, and Labour is going to have to fight to hold every one of the unusual gains it made in 1997. Although Labour is no longer a socialist party – and the flavour of politics is more reminiscent of that during the Liberal-Conservative conflict of the Edwardian era than of anything seen since – there is no reason to suspect, at this stage, that the electoral map of England has changed permanently. Labour's worst fear must be that there will be a reversion to type, and that the norm in England, even with Wales still represented in the English parliament and dominated by Labour, would be more or less permanent Conservative administration once England were decoupled from Scotland.

If the Labour party gets itself into a mess as a result of its commitment to devolution, it needs to ask itself: what did we expect would happen? The establishment of little pockets of government, whether in Scotland or in Wales, was what was meant by 'devolution'. Labour, unfortunately, never realised what sort of governing those little pockets would aspire to do. It did not recognise what hopes would be fuelled by such measures of self-rule as it was, in its radical constitution-breaking, prepared to grant. Labour seemed to make the breaking-up of the United Kingdom an implicit goal of its entire constitutional policy. Almost everybody outside the Labour party came to realise this but, surprisingly, almost no one inside it. Indeed, it has been a consistent theme of the first two years of this administration that it has not been able to see, or will not see, the logical conclusions to which its attempts to change the constitution inexorably lead.

The pursuit of devolution, like the equally ill-judged fascination for proportional representation that has become a commensurate obsession for a few members of the Labour party, can in the end have only one outcome: the prevention of Labour from exercising any meaningful power. In conceiving its obsession with constitutional reform, Labour was apparently saying: we no longer want to be bothered to have to govern anywhere serious, where real power resides and where real influence can be had in the world; we would rather do things on a smaller scale. In the hubris the party experienced not just after its election victory in 1997, but in the couple of years beforehand as it coasted towards triumph, it became forgetful of reality. It knew it would govern Britain; but it could not see that as it spewed out promises of devolution here, or of electoral reform there, that it was helping to ensure it could not govern in that way indefinitely. As a political force, it was signing its own death warrant by being so free with its promises of reform. This insouciance might have been understandable to an extent if Labour had felt it could rely upon having the government of England as a consolation prize; but it cannot. Indeed, the very notion that there might one day, soon, have to be something called 'the government of England' was never dreamt of in Labour's philosophy.

The honour of forming such a government, should it become necessary, would in any normal circumstances fall to the Conservative party. At almost every general election this century the Conservatives have had a majority of the seats in England. However, this was not so in 1997, and it is unlikely to be so until the Conservative party can bring itself to do something other than an impersonation of a pantomime horse with a head at either end. Just how soon normal service will be resumed in that party it is impossible to say. All the signs are that, whatever certain self-deluded leading Conservatives might think, the general public still feel that the party is an abortion, its policies incoherent and its personnel repellent. It is hard to conceive of the level of incompetence and dishonesty the present Labour government would have to accomplish before even the most broad-minded of floating voters would wish to place his trust in the Conservatives.

There are various policies, attitudes and wheezes that the Conservatives could try in the hope of rebuilding themselves in the affections of the English people. Yet, as one might expect, the Conservatives have been predictably slow to see the opportunity with which their present catastrophe in Scotland has presented them. Without having to make any agonising decisions to this effect, they are magically already an English party. The unhappy reasons for this need not be dwelt upon. They are in the past. What is important – and, sadly, this still has not happened – is for the Conservatives to recognise that, in this respect at least, there is no turning back the clock. It may well be that in fifty or one hundred years' time the Scots will love the Conservative party. It may well be that there will, one day, be another Act of Union, and that England and Scotland will realise that, for all sorts of reasons, they belong together, and by mutual consent they once more come together. Until and unless that day comes, there is no point the Conservative party fantasising about its having an important role in Scotland and Wales. If it wishes to maximise its potential as a party interested in, and perhaps even one day again exercising, power, then its foremost priority must be to establish itself as an English nationalist party.

It is felt dangerous in politics to be right too soon. The politicians' graveyard is full of people who argued, thirty years ago, about the merits of what was then called denationalisation, or what even a Labour Chancellor of the Exchequer now admires as monetarism. Yet on the question of English sensibilities, it is probably not too soon for the Conservatives to be right. They should have recognised that there is a constituency in England of English who have heard loud and clear what the Scots have to say to them. They might not all have heard it couched in the fierce language of *Trainspotting*, but they are given to understand that in the eyes and hearts of many of the Scottish people, the English have served their, mainly economic, purpose. Any political party that says to the English, 'Look, we shall take notice of these realities, and be ready to advance to the English people a range of policies that will benefit their interests in the event of Scotland becoming independent', could well, quite soon, find it has had that most elusive of political assets: the 'big idea'.

Having been completely wiped out, in parliamentary terms, in Scotland and Wales, the Conservatives ought by now to have received this message loud and clear. However, like so many English males, they simply do not know when to take no for an answer. Have they, bless them, looked at the opinion polls conducted in Scotland since their débâcle on 1 May 1997, and noticed how their hitherto pathetic level of support is still bumping along the bottom? Have they not worked out, despite their cynical attempts to make the Scottish Conservative Party as separate an entity as possible since 1997, that few in Scotland appear to be taken in? Perhaps once the Conservatives succeed in getting some representation in the Edinburgh parliament –

which, thanks to the absence of a first-past-the-post system for the Scottish elections, even they should do – then they will have a platform from which to convince us that Scottish Conservatism and English Conservatism are not quite the same thing. That distinction might, in turn, win them more adherents north of the border, especially if Scotland has a broadly socialist hegemony in control of it that drives those more liberal electors who do not wish to emigrate to England to look for an alternative. However, Conservatives in both England and Scotland need to accept that this means of making Conservatism popular once more in Scotland entails recognition that these are two separate countries, with two separate political and social cultures. It means the Conservative party acknowledging that it should let its people in Scotland develop their policies entirely free of control from the party in England, and therefore owning up to the realities of the separatist movement.

Having thus tailored Conservatism to Scottish needs, and therefore ceased worrying about how to reconcile predominantly English Conservative values with the milder version that would be likely to appeal to many Scots, the separate English party could then quite easily direct itself to the cause of encouraging support in England. The party seems to shy away from English nationalism for the usual reasons – the distant sound of jackboots, imaginings of bonkers theories of racial superiority, and all that other nonsense. Only a few nutters in England identify with their country in that sort of way, and there is no need to appeal to them. What the English Conservative party needs to do is to judge those policies that the English like, and which are commensurate with the basic tenets of Toryism, and give them to the English. In the past, that could only be done at the risk of offending those parts of the kingdom where a different political and social culture obtained, notably Scotland. Now, if only the Conservatives had the foresight, boldness and imagination to restructure themselves in the light of the realities, that risk need no longer be there.

The Conservatives have done this before. Thatcherism was a creed that naturally had more appeal to the English than to the Scots. Although, in reality, there were only marginal differences between the affluence of Scotland and that of England, there was a love of statism and welfarism in Scotland that made the Thatcherite message inherently unpalatable to many Scots. We have already noted the paradox inherent in this, that the message was essentially one invented by one of the greatest Scotsmen of all, Adam Smith, 225 years ago. Perhaps if Smith had been alive to enunciate his message of free markets and their link with personal liberty, to speak to his fellow countrymen in tones they recognised and understood, there would not have been a problem. Regrettably, he was not; and it is hard to imagine three people more antipathetic to the Scots than Mrs Thatcher herself, Sir Geoffrey Howe and Nigel Lawson, who were the three ministers who undertook most of the articulation of the gospel of Thatcherism to the world.

The English, of course, loved it. It was an act of irresponsibility for someone to invent the stereotype of Essex Man, but that stereotype did at least exemplify the differences, as a matter of general principle, between the Scots and the English. For a start, many of the most lucrative financial opportunities in the 1980s were to be had in England, notably in London and the South-east. In the context in which they were available, everything was possible. The philosophy of self-help seemed as though it was about to supersede that of welfarism, though the devil never did quite take the hindmost. In many spheres – such as housing and pensions – private ownership steadily replaced state provision. Capitalism grew unchecked, as capitalism should; the only limit placed on the amount of money that could be earned in certain trades was the amount of time the worker was prepared to spend earning it. By the end of the 1980s some of the Scots had worked themselves into an unfortunate mentality, that of the little boy whose nose is pressed to the window of the sweetshop: only they were under the impression that the shopkeeper was taunting them through the half-open door about not pulling themselves together and becoming wealthy enough to afford the merchandise.

How far this was perception, and how far reality, is a matter for conjecture. The economic statistics about Scotland's success during the Thatcher years suggest that things were not nearly so bad as the Scots might have imagined. However much many of them hated the aggressively capitalist culture of Thatcherism, they too practised it in some measure, and derived benefits from it. The Scots also had the opportunity for a wallow in *Schadenfreude* when the recession, induced by what the late and lamented Jock Bruce-Gardyne called Nigel Lawson's 'legover with the Deutschmark' followed by the near-suicidal entry of sterling into the ERM, impoverished many of those customers who had been regulars in the sweetshop. The English might suspect that it was not so much what the Scots were being asked to do that upset them about the English, but the accent and the tone in which they were being asked to do it.

VI

Since we live in a parliamentary democracy – though one in which the whore of the referendum is all too often these days plying her trade – the people who give voice to the notion of the reinvention of England ought best to be a political party. If, suddenly, England is left on its own after the end of the affair with Scotland, someone is going to have to be in charge of the project of convincing the English that this is not the end of the world, that there is life after the repeal or abrogation of the Act of Union. However adept that party has become at reversals of principle, such a message would look odd coming from

Labour – even though English independence, if it comes about, would be entirely their fault. Since the Conservatives now find themselves *de facto* the party of England, and since after any normal election they ought to expect to command a majority of English seats, they are the best placed to have first stab at masterminding the project. It remains, however, a slow and painful process to persuade them to realise this. If they display incompetence and lack of decisiveness on this of all issues, then the English people are unlikely to be especially forgiving. In short, making a mess of this situation, and failing to articulate the true wishes of the English people at what would be a time of trial and uncertainty, could ensure that they do not govern again for a generation.

The fact is that if the Conservative party blows such an opportunity as would be presented to them by a decision by the Scots to become independent – if it shows, in those circumstances, that it cannot even connect with its own heartland anymore – then it might just as well pack up and let someone else organise on the right. It is important that the party realises why it lost the 1997 election. It did terribly badly in England not because the message that had so attracted English voters in the 1980s was now offensive to them: it was because the Conservatives themselves, with their inadequate prime minister and a collection of his colleagues who, to put it politely, should have had the regular attentions of a probation officer, were now personally offensive to the people. The Labour party only did so well by adopting much of the agenda that had appealed to English Conservatives, and presenting it as their own. If this is thought to be an exaggeration, it ought to be noted that the various resemblances between New Labour and English Conservatism have undeniably caused that party to take its dive in the Scottish opinion polls. Mr Salmond's speeches are, after all, full of his regret and anger at the adoption of so much ultra-Conservative economic practice by Mr Brown.

This cultural divide stands at the Conservatives' service.

They, unlike Labour, do not any longer have to pretend to appease the whole of the British Isles the whole of the time. They can go forward advocating tax-cutting policies for the benefit of the English that will be made possible by the end of the subsidy to Scotland. They can talk of freeing up funds that currently are poured into the unproductive sectors of the Scottish economy being diverted, instead, to the productive sectors of the economy in England. They can speak, albeit cynically, of the benefits likely to flow to England by the establishment of an old-style, high-taxing, socialist regime in Scotland. They can tailor their manifesto in all respects to a country in which rulers and ruled speak the same language, understand the same idioms, and have an identical culture. The sensibilities of pampered minorities (to use a phrase that Tories of a more violent sort would love to be able to deploy) would no longer have to be taken into consideration. In short, those in England who would like someone to stand up for their interests as English people – someone not from the lunatic fringes of politics, but who instead embodied the traditional moderate and anti-statist virtues of English political culture – would find themselves catered for. It would be a happy moment for everyone in the Conservative cause.

It is, though, Conservativism that is the home of lost causes these days. It was within the Conservative heart that the last fantasies of empire and the imperial role were harboured during the 1960s, and at such great financial and emotional cost. It will, it appears, be in that same heart that the fantasies of a United Kingdom are nursed, long after the Scots have made clear what they think of their English paymasters and landlords. There are signs that fewer and fewer Conservatives are actually labouring under similar delusions now, but it will still be a sticky process for them to disengage romantically from Scotland. The present leader of the Conservative party has been at pains not to paint his party as an English nationalist enterprise; perhaps he feels he has too many other battles to fight at the moment.

He talks, instead, of the possibilities of an English parliament as part of a federal system, an idea with which we shall deal in the final part of this tract. This all means that the English political party best suited by temperament and popular support to identify itself with the new needs of an independent England, and to shape with some sincerity and understanding the sort of humane, non-aggressive nationalism that England would want in order to flourish, looks like missing the proverbial bus. With the other English political parties in a state of even more advanced pretence that Scottish separation is never going to happen, it looks as though the English people – not for the first time – will be lacking the sort of leadership they should have a right to expect. It must be hoped that this failure of the political class will be rectified before something even more unpleasant than the existing parties comes along to fill the vacuum, or before England is forced to stumble, uncertainly, into what ought to be a glowing future. A map will be needed, so let us try to provide our rulers with one.

THREE

The Rights of Majorities

If there is such a thing as an English national trait – and it is
dangerous to make such assumptions – then it must be cheer-
fulness, or optimism: what our parents' generation called 'the
Dunkirk spirit'. It does not just mean turning apparent defeat
into victory, though there would be an element of that in the
calculations the English ought to make should the Scots choose
independence. It also means believing that the English nation
can carry on much as it has since the Conquest, whether part
of some wider association or not, and that the English people
can (like their Scottish cousins) find a community of interest
together for the future. We should be optimistic on this count,
as well as on that issue discussed in the last part: that there will
be the political leadership, eventually, to steer the English safely,
happily and undramatically into any future that they have to
face on their own. However inept our main political parties are,
it is hard to believe that there are not in all of them plenty of
people interested in power, and who recognise just what a
repository of power England would remain after Scottish independence. If these people really are any good at politics, they
will proceed to fill the vacuum themselves, displaying the
opportunism that has for so long characterised their trade.
What, though, must the new governors of England seek to do
when the time comes to draw up the plan of how England,
shorn of Scotland, must be governed?

We have, it is to be hoped, settled that England has no excuse not to summon the moral and psychological will to accept that it can survive and flourish if Scotland chooses to break the Union, and the United Kingdom. Equally, it must be clear that, whatever the sentimental difficulties, the financial consequences of such a break can only be good for England, and that the challenges presented to the self-interest of England's political parties will not be insuperable. Although many will still find the idea of an independent England unthinkable or mad, if it happens there will be no escape from the fact that it has happened. If the Scots choose separation, it cannot be stressed enough that the first responsibility of the English would be to stop fretting about it, and instead to design a satisfactory form of government for themselves.

This process would involve settling what sort of institutions would be used to govern England, and how they would be different – if very much at all – from those that currently govern the United Kingdom. Also, some sort of political lead ought to be given in the question of the new identity of England and the English people – though knowing the individualism, and the desire to be left alone by the state, which is rooted in the English mentality, the English will prefer for the most part to sort that out for themselves, rather than having it dictated too overtly by their government. By simply carrying on as they have before, the English people would project their own values both nationally and internationally. However, with an independent Scotland making its own mark in the world, it will soon become clear, without any real conscious effort by the English, what the English voice and the English temper are – and how they might in some respects be distinct from the British ones to which we, and the world, have become so used. We should not forget, either, that at such a time the newly independent Scots would be projecting themselves to the world in their own way, an act which would in itself accentuate the difference of England.

It is in considering this last point that we must confront head-on the alternative to England's being a distinct nation after the break-up of the United Kingdom. This is the move to which so many in the British political class – English as well as Scottish – are wedded, of reducing the constituent parts of what is presently the United Kingdom to the level of small, regionally defined satrapies of Brussels. There is the hope, long expressed from the European centre, of there being a Europe of the regions; those who support the European project in England would naturally hope for an England of the regions that could slot into that new superstate with ease. That superstate can exist only once national identities are submerged; and breaking up nations into regions is an ideal means of doing this (another of the many paradoxes not appreciated by the 'Scotland Independent in Europe' brigade). In the end, the survival of an independent England may well depend on the English finally overcoming the threat to their nationhood posed by the European Union, and resisting the unhistorical notion of regionalism. There is no cause for England to leave, or threaten to leave, the European Union, though there are many arguments, not relevant here, about why it should never rule out the option of doing so. However, for its own sake it must see to it that its membership is based on the idea of the European Union as a community of free-trading nation states, even if some of the other members are less keen on that idea than the English are. Having that mentality rooted at the start of England's independence would be the most helpful attitude for the future.

Even before the time comes for the English people to embark upon the debate about their new institutions, they should remember one important point about the political class whose responsibility it will ultimately be to settle them. The key to reforming any constitution in a democracy – that is to say, in any country where it has not been traditional to change such arrangements with the help of the armed forces, terrorism or popular revolution – is to try to pretend that many of those people whose constitution is being reformed will be largely or completely unaffected or disadvantaged by it. Successive British governments have been aware of this, and have operated on that basis – it is why the West Lothian Question was dismissed by the Callaghan government, and why the present Labour administration could not own up to the likely consequences of devolution. Human nature being what it is, it is not hard to see why. The Scots and the Welsh provided quite enough trouble, with their constant demands for devolution. Had the English leapt on the bandwagon too, government would have been about nothing other than the internal squabbles of the tribes within a supposedly united kingdom. It was far better to pretend that the English, not being a minority, had none of the special rights that the government was all too ready to accord to the Scots and Welsh. Therefore, throughout this whole current process of devolution – and it was as true in the 1970s as it has been in the 1990s – the English have not been accorded the same rights and privileges as those granted to the Scots and Welsh. The English have not, as has been noted, had their opinions tested in a referendum. It is as if the very fact of being in a majority somehow removes any obligation on a government to treat those in the majority with any constitutional respect.

Pending Scotland's finally choosing to be independent, this disadvantage to the English continues. It is a wrong that cries out to be righted immediately, as a preliminary step to the possible need the English may soon have to assert England's rights as a properly independent country. The halfway house of devolution allows the Scots their own parliament and continuing representation – or, rather, over-representation – at Westminster. What is more, there seems to be the traditional great reluctance among the English to get up and complain about their being taken for a ride in this way. It is not just that the Scots, under the present Labour government, have an unfair preponderance in the affairs of England: it is that they continue to benefit unduly, to the tune of about £8 billion a year or a quarter of all that is spent by the British state in Scotland, from the enforced generosity of the English taxpayer. Given that Scotland is imminently to have its own parliament, with only major strategic matters remaining to be decided at Westminster, it is not only hard to see why that country should continue to be over-represented in the British parliament; it is hard to see why it merits even equal representation per head of the population compared with England, given that the English have no parliament of their own. Allowing the Scots to have, say, two-thirds the number of elected MPs per head of their population compared with England would seem a generous interim solution. However, the Labour government has, for the usual electoral reasons, been reluctant to talk about a timetable for scaling down representation. Its spokesmen have also made it clear that there can be no question of that representation, once the question is finally addressed, being anything less than on a par with England's. It can only be that so few English are aware of this injustice, and of the intention of the government to perpetuate it, that there has not been a sustained outcry about it.

These plans for representation would, if implemented, be both illogical and, like many illogical things, unfair. The English would be represented in just one parliament; the Scots, until such times as they chose to become independent, in two. No sensible case – no case that rests on anything other than the ruthless and cynical securing of political advantage – can be made for the Scots, if they must be represented in both parliaments, being over-represented in the one in which they are a minority interest; and to be represented on equal terms with a country that has only one parliament would constitute flagrant over-representation. There is no reason why the English should have to tolerate the presence of Scots MPs in such large numbers in the English parliament, bringing their influence to bear either on matters that do not concern them, or having undue and disproportionate influence on matters that do.

Indeed, it is patronising to the Scots in the extreme to treat them in this way, and they themselves should, in return for the new democratic rights just granted them, be the first to campaign for fairer representation.

There is, as we observed in the last part, only one reason why the Labour party should be so reluctant to see lower representation in Scotland, and that is the extent to which it usually depends on Scottish MPs to bolster its parliamentary party. It is only in the parliament elected in 1997, and the one elected in 1945, that Labour would ever have been able to govern if it had had no Scots MPs. If Welsh representation were reduced to recognise the fact of the Welsh assembly, matters would be tighter still. England currently has 529 parliamentary seats, so Labour would need to win 265 to govern with a bare majority if elections were ever confined to an English parliament alone. In the freak year of 1997 they won 328, but cannot (despite the superlative and continuing efforts of the Conservative party to assist them) bank on such an achievement being repeated.

In their armoury for resisting the demands of the English – should the English ever acquire the political consciousness to make any demands, that is – Labour has long had the weapon of regional assemblies. The *quid pro quo* for the Scots having their parliament and the Welsh their assembly, while still having undue representation in what ought to be the English parliament at Westminster, is that England should have regional assemblies. Why? How would this make the government of England any better? How would it negate the fundamental injustice of so many Scots having a say in the running of England at the parliamentary level? And what is a region? What purpose would these assemblies serve? Or would they just help the Labour party shore up its own power, for the time being, at the expense of another layer of costly bureaucracy without which England can function perfectly well? Might it be that the campaign for regional assemblies has nothing to do with equalising the democratic rights of the English with those of the Scots, Welsh and Northern Irish? Might this campaign, instead, be simply part of the obsessive desire by much of the political class to eradicate the notion of nationhood, and all its ancient relevances, first from Great Britain, and then from England? And can there be any connection between this obsession and what the people of England, if they were ever asked about the matter, would themselves really want?

II

The decision to have an elected mayor, with a small assembly, for Greater London has been hailed by some as the first great blow for regionalism. At the moment, the idea has widespread popular support, though that in itself might be a legacy of the hatred of the last Conservative government, which abolished the Greater London Council in 1986 and was long opposed to the notion of a London mayoralty. The idea may be less popular once a mayor is actually elected, and once London's new governing body is seen in operation. The Greater London area is also a distinct part of the country, and it unarguably has special needs, given the magnetic effect that London has in relation to the rest of the South-east, and to tourists and visitors from the world over; though it is hard to see what the people of, say, Pinner have in common with those of Plaistow, other than hoping for an improved level of service on the London Underground. It would hardly be so easy to convince the people of, say, Essex, Suffolk, Norfolk and Cambridgeshire that they needed an authority to look after them as East Anglians; or that Wessex should be similarly favoured; or working out where one part of the Midlands ends, and another one begins. One of the problems with being an old country – and being an old country is perhaps the most obvious fact about England, yet one to which constitutional progressives are wilfully, and painfully, oblivious – is that English people have definite local allegiances: witness the rare acts of English political consciousness that led to Avon becoming part of Somerset, or Hull becoming part of Yorkshire again, or Rutland being reborn. Ask a man from Newcastle-upon-Tyne what he is and he will tell you he is a Geordie, not a north-easterner.

We can never, though, escape that more insidious reason for the cult of regionalism. Breaking up the nation of the United Kingdom is easily done, for it has its distinct components. In theory, each of those components – even possibly Wales, given a superhuman effort and sufficiently lavish European subsidy – is strong enough in its self-identification to have the will to survive. Regionalism is, in the eyes of those who fear either English nationalism or nationalism *tout court*, the perfect anti-dote to and subversive of those creeds. The English, at the time when they become an independent nation again, will be strangely vulnerable in this regard. If, before the English have properly stopped thinking of themselves as British, they could instead make the leap to consider themselves West Coun-trymen, East Anglians or Midlanders, Brussels would be saved a great deal of trouble in its enduring project to obliterate national consciousness. It is only if the English, with their 50 million people, their historic borders once more resignified and their institutions revived, intervene to prevent such an unnecessary process as regionalisation that Brussels would encounter a new and painful obstacle in its drive towards a superstate.

There is no doubt that the Europeans are gearing up to exploit, in this way, a moment of vulnerability, such as the English might suffer when and if Scotland breaks away from the Union. There can be no guarantee (indeed, the evidence is sadly to the contrary) that the English would be any more resistant to the sight of the Eurochequebook than the Scots intend to be. This moral turpitude would make the English intensely vulnerable to regionalism. It is entirely possible that subsidies to the English regions from Brussels – of which there is a distinguished history, as the sponsorship signs alongside various stretches of new English roads, for example, have made clear in the last few years – could be increasingly used as bribes in much the same way as they are with the Scots. There would, however, be a difference. In Scotland, such bribes are being used to help sunder an already distinct entity from its geographical and political partner, and to create a new client relationship with an emerging, but already powerful, ultimate authority. In England, the bribes would have to be used to fragment an already distinct entity whose borders and coherence are steeped in historical precedent. Nonetheless, money talks, and it might help make an eloquent case for regionalism at a time when the English are feeling especially unconfident about their nationhood.

An aggressive political lead would have to be given to a policy of regionalism in England for it to have any chance of success. A propaganda campaign, accompanying a fundamental restructuring of England, would be needed to imprint what the government decided were the new constitutional realities on the English people. First, the British government (for this would, of course, be undertaken as a 'sop' to the English in the period after the Scots had obtained their devolved parliament and before any decision was taken to become independent) would need to have a policy of establishing regional assemblies in England and of designing responsibilities for those assemblies, breaking them away from central government and county councils. The British parliament would then have to approve such a move – with the help, perhaps, of Scottish MPs, none of whose business this would be, but who were still allowed to interfere in it anyway. Once the regions were established, the people who lived there would be encouraged to think regionally by all manner of propaganda, and by the well-publicised news that beefy financial grants were being made direct to the regions from Brussels and Westminster. Unless the people were alerted to the true purpose and likely consequences of this violation of their history and were prepared to resist it through the political process, England would soon cease to cohere; and there would be no reason why, to accompany the devolution of powers downwards from these assemblies, various of Westminster's remaining powers should not be devolved upward to the controllers of the superstate, making England an irrelevant concept altogether. Those who imagine that there will always be some things that a national parliament – whether an English one, or a federal abomination such as we shall consider in a moment – would have to do, such as defence, foreign and economic policy are simply not looking at the map. It all depends what one thinks is meant by the term 'European Union'. What those driving the train think it means is giving the English a taste of how the Scots have felt since 1707.

III

The Conservative party was responsible, during its last period in government, for establishing a regional strategic structure, mainly at Brussels' behest. Those ministers who participated in this wasteful exercise and who encouraged it most assiduously were mainly from the pro-European wing of the party. The exercise showed once more the party's peculiar abilities of money-wasting, and its supreme disregard for the structural and constitutional consequences of its political actions. Now, some in the Conservative movement have become alert to the dangers of regionalism, and to the likelihood of there being difficulties consequent upon the fragmentation of the United Kingdom. They have, therefore, come up with what they consider to be the perfect antidote to this threat. Seeing the Scots, Welsh and Ulstermen having their own talking-shops, they want one too. They talk of an English parliament; one that will not take the place of the United Kingdom parliament at

Westminster, but would complement it. In their fantasies, the United Kingdom parliament still meets occasionally to discuss matters of United Kingdom legislation, on matters such as defence and foreign policy; but all those parochial things that, under devolution, are to be done in Scotland by the Scottish parliament would in future be done in England by the English parliament.

Now, this would without question achieve one aim of the English nationalists, namely to have the Scots removed from any influence over English affairs in the same way that the Scots have removed the English from consideration of their affairs. However, what the enthusiasts for such a scheme cannot see is that such a move would be the first triumph of regionalism. It would not be a parliament for the English nation in the true sense, because the things that matter most of all to a nation of 50 million people – its economic management, its taxation, its defence and its foreign relations – would still not be matters for English determination. In seeking what they regard as equal treatment for England, the advocates of this parliament equate England with Scotland. The ludicrousness of such a comparison does not, it seems, occur to them. It may be all very well to set up a parliament for five million people and to say that that parliament cannot discuss important national questions, for they will continue to be discussed and decided elsewhere (though the SNP is not happy at that). To do it to a nation of 50 million people that is still, for all its faults and precipitate modern decline, one of the most powerful and significant nations on earth, is unreal. That some of high rank and former distinction in the Conservative movement can even con- template such a thing provides further proof that that organ- isation is rotting from the head down.

By all means let there be an English parliament: but let us see St George's flag flying permanently over the Victoria tower at Westminster, and not hauled down one day a week to make way for the discredited and pointless sham of the Union flag that would signify the sitting of the 'federal' parliament. The only English parliament worth having is one that has the authority to deal with all questions affecting the English nation. It would include Members of Parliament from all constituencies in the land of England, as well as from England's dependencies in Ulster and Wales for so long as a majority in those places chose not to seek independence. Quite clearly, such a worthwhile parliament cannot exist at the same time as a British federal entity. A British federal entity could last only so long as there was no independent Scotland, and would be a standing rebuke to the English in the impotence it would impose upon England.

Our knowledge of history tells us why so many in the Conservative movement (and I use that term rather than 'Conservative party' because so many who consider themselves Conservatives would not be seen dead actually joining or supporting the party under its present management) are attracted by the half-baked idea of an English parliament as part of a federal structure. It is a way, as they see it, of standing up for English interests while maintaining the soothing illusion of some sort of Union. In other words, it is our old friend blind sentimentality yet again interfering with reality and common sense. These Conservatives – who in any other context drone on about the importance of cutting public spending and bureaucracy – are quite happy when it comes to this question of inventing yet another tier of government and having yet another group of self-important, mediocre people who cannot find a proper job come in to run it for them. It is another reminder of how, whenever it comes to settling the important questions of how we are governed, the political class has always to deal first with the even more important question of how it is to be employed.

There is, though, one alarming point that needs to be considered before we bury the idea of the English (federal) parliament under the ton of ridicule it merits. If Scotland chooses to become independent, then the English will *de facto* get their parliament; and it will be the proper parliament of the representatives of 50 million people, discussing the affairs that matter to them, and not a glorified county council representing the triumph of European regionalism. It will be a parliament in which 50 million English can be represented, and in which their representatives alone will judge and vote upon issues that affect them alone. But what if Scotland chooses not to become independent?

In that case, the present unsatisfactory arrangements, of Scotland's having two lots of representation and having the right to interfere in English affairs, will be seen to be perpetuated indefinitely. So, too, will the status of the Scottish parliament as a body whose main interest and function is to continue to prise substantial amounts of money out of the United Kingdom parliament, acting as the middle man between Scotland and the English taxpayer. At this point, when the English realise that these injustices are to be inflicted upon them for an indefinite period, even they will turn ugly. Even their limited levels of political consciousness will be stimulated to the point where they protest. It is, regrettably, at that juncture when the misguided advocates of that English (federal) parliament will sense that their moment has come.

It does not, though, need to be like that. As a first step, the rejection by Scotland of the option of full independence – either by a failure of the electorate to support the SNP in the forthcoming Scottish elections or, having supported the SNP, to reject independence when it is put to them in a referendum – must be taken as the clear sign by the English that certain abuses of their good nature cannot continue indefinitely. However emasculated it may be, the Conservative party needs to argue for immediate legislation to reduce the level of Scottish representation in parliament. This might seem a futile pursuit given the size of Labour's majority; but the Labour party is not stupid when it comes to gauging public opinion, and even it must recognise that being seen to impede the will of the English people by acting unjustly towards them is unlikely to guarantee it great success at a subsequent general election.

Even if Labour recognised that its own self-interest depended on its making such a concession to logic and fairness, there would still be one glaring illogicality and unfairness. The West Lothian Question would still not have had a proper answer. There have been suggestions that, on any given division in the House of Commons, the Speaker should be able to adjudge whether the matter is a United Kingdom one or one confined to matters affecting England. If it were the latter, a ruling could be made that only English MPs might speak in the debate and take part in the division. This in itself would be a regrettable step, for it would make a mockery of parliament in its present form, and of parliament's historic conventions. It is also alarmingly close to the solution to the West Lothian Question laid out by Sir Edward Heath, and therefore it should give us all pause for thought. However, this regrettable step may yet be necessitated by the subversion of the British constitution that the devolution arrangements put before the Scottish people in the 1997 referendum represent.

However, even after these changes, dissatisfaction would continue among the English. The economy would still be a matter for the sham of the United Kingdom parliament. It can be regarded as certain that the power granted to the Scottish parliament to vary the basic rate of income tax by 3 per cent would not be used to the full to compensate for the voluntary refusal of the English subsidy. In any case, raising an extra three pence in the pound from Scottish taxpayers would come nowhere near covering the £8 billion pumped in annually by the English. The English would feel, with some justification, that they were still being taken advantage of. The very activities of the Scottish parliament would be a forcible, continuing reminder to the English that they had never been asked about whether they were happy to pay such a large subsidy to a country that had succeeded in extracting a substantial measure of independence from them. So perhaps, after all, the notion of a referendum among the English, about whether they would like to become independent from Scotland, might not be a bad idea: it might not be so otiose as we thought. No doubt some interesting propaganda could be furnished to the public by those masterminding the pro-independence campaign, featuring not merely the details of the great financial bonanza awaiting the English once the dependent relative's chains were taken off their country, but also quoting lavishly (if the Obscene Publications Act allows) from that reflective soliloquy in *Trainspotting*. The fundamental point is this: that for so long as Scotland is seen to enjoy constitutional and political favours that are not only denied to the English, but which are provided and paid for by them to some extent, then the sensibilities of the English will be offended, and the present relationship between the two countries will deteriorate. Removing this imbalance means either ending devolution or ending the Union. Given the Pandora's Box nature of all politics, the first is impossible; the second may not just be the wish of a growing number of Scots, but might also become the increasing desire of many of the more perceptive English.

IV

The difficulty of sustaining the 1997 devolution settlement indefinitely, though, would become apparent only if the Scots were to stop following the apparently logical, and for all we know inevitable, course upon which they are now well embarked. If they carry on in the way they are going, the English will be faced with four very different questions. The first would be about how the existing British institutions would need to be adapted by the English to govern a country that has been separated from Scotland. The second would be about the basis on which England should establish its relations with the newly independent Scots. The third would be about whether existing British policies on issues such as foreign affairs or defence would need to be adapted to reflect especially English sensibilities. The fourth would concern what practical steps should be taken to make the English conscious of their nationality, and to encourage them to express their Englishness in a pacific, constructive and tolerant way.

In working out how England best governs itself as an independent country, the subtraction method is the logical place to start. We considered earlier how we find an English identity, after all these years of being British, by simply working out what is left once the Scots have gone. It would not be very different; the English have, inevitably, carried on being English all the time they thought they were actually being British. It is the same with English institutions, most of which were expanded to serve Britain at the time of the Act of Union, or have in other ways been adapted accordingly. Now, those institutions could be contracted or unadapted. Assuming Wales and the Six Counties were still represented in the English parliament once Scotland had become independent, the House of Commons at Westminster would suddenly find it had 587 MPs instead of 659. Consideration would then, as I have noted earlier, have to be given to the nature of Ulster's and Wales's representation. The Welsh could not have their assembly and forty MPs. If they must have the former – and, with Scotland gone, there would be much less call for it – then their representation at Westminster should be cut by a third, or thirteen seats. As for the assembly, the cession of Scotland from the Union would provide the perfect opportunity to have another referendum in Wales. There is no reason not to give the Welsh the opportunity that both they and the Scots should, in an ideal world, have been given in 1997: to allow them to choose complete independence. They would not, of course, choose it, whatever the fantasists of 'The Party of Wales' might imagine, but it would be decent of the English to give them the opportunity.

Having, we must presume, answered 'no' to the first question, the Welsh could then be asked a second: about whether, in the light of the experience, they could see any point in continuing with the assembly they voted by so narrow a margin, and on so low a turnout, to establish in 1997. If they answered 'yes', they should be warned that this, too, would serve only to stoke up enmity among the English about the preferential treatment being given to the Welsh in matters of government. It would not be good for Wales's long-term relations with England for it to become a permanent drain on the English taxpayer while being over-represented in the English parliament. It would lead, in the first instance, to a demand by the English for the sort of reduction in Welsh representation at Westminster that has been suggested above. For the Welsh to want to have their cake and eat it in this respect might in the end prompt the English to ask, one day, to be consulted about their feelings towards Wales, just as they ought to have been asked about whether they wished to continue funding Scotland in a relationship whose terms come to be dictated more and more by the dependent.

Ulster's representation in the English parliament is an issue complicated by the violent and bigoted forces at work in the Six Counties, and which successive British governments have chosen to appease rather than to confront. Since the British political parties have, between them, rejected the correct course for Ulster – which was to have it governed in the same way as any other part of the pre-devolution Great Britain, with its laws made in parliament and not by Order in Council – then there can be no excuse for Ulster's having eighteen seats in the English parliament. Its old level of twelve MPs, as in the days of Stormont, would seem to be fair. However, this is a decision that would not need to be taken until Scotland left the United Kingdom, ended it as a political entity, and left England with its own parliament. If by some miracle the assembly established in Ulster at the elections of June 1998 has survived for that long, then there will be no need to maintain such a level of representation in England's parliament. However, the notions of independence that are so real in Scotland, and so harmlessly wild in Wales, cannot, as we have noted earlier, be entertained in the unusual climate of Ulster. That province's representation in the English parliament is likely to remain a necessity for some time, to help guarantee the rights of a majority there who wish to remain under the protection of the English, or British, Crown.

There is no reason, once England has established its own parliament with the appropriate representation from its dependencies – which may even, for all we know, include Shetland too – why Westminster cannot carry on much as before. There will be no Scottish Grand Committee, of course, but all the rest of the panoply of accountability can continue uninterrupted. Such changes as might once have been necessary in the House of Lords, such as the removal from those holding Scottish peerages of their rights to sit, speak and vote there, are now likely not to be needed. The legislation now in train to strip hereditary peers of their voting rights – and since no Scottish peerage has been created since the Act of Union, all holders of such peerages today do so by hereditary right – will do for these peers in any case. Any Scots who continue to sit in the Lords will do so by virtue of a modern United Kingdom life peerage.

There is, though, the interesting question of the status of United Kingdom peerages were the United Kingdom to cease to exist. Most United Kingdom peers are English and would therefore expect to sit in an English parliament. Where, though, would this leave Scots who have been given United Kingdom peerages, of whom there are many? If the House of Lords were just to be a harmless revising chamber, then the presence there of Scotsmen and women, however offensive to logic, would not really be offensive to anything else. The effort of remaking such a house in the light of Scottish separatism would hardly be worth the trouble. However, now that the House of Lords is, in the view of the Labour government, to be given greater legitimacy by having the hereditary element removed, then it would matter much more who sits there: for with this supposed (but, in fact, entirely bogus) greater legitimacy would come greater power. Should this new quango be properly established, it would seek to be the sort of second chamber we see in other countries, even though in the first instance there are no plans to elect any of its members, but simply to include the beneficiaries of recent patronage. The new House of Lords might even, one day, start asking why, as a supposedly legitimate second chamber, it should not have some of the powers vested in those in other democracies, such as a right of veto over some of the ridiculous things done by the House of Commons. In that case, the status of those who sit in such a chamber would take on a new significance. It is plain, therefore, that should Scotland become independent, those peers who took Scottish citizenship would have to forfeit their right to sit in the English House of Lords.

It is not just peers of the realm with an allegiance to Scotland who would need to consider their positions after the partition of Great Britain. The new realities would affect everyone who might have cause to consider himself or herself Scottish. A mistake, of sentimental origins and offensive in logic, was made with the treatment of Irish Free State, later Irish Republic, citizens after the partition of Ireland. They were, and still are, allowed unlimited rights of access to the United Kingdom, enjoying full civil rights even to the extent of voting in British elections, and benefiting from the British social security system. There is no call to perpetuate this, even now we are both members of the same European Union. The final fragmentation of the Union with Scotland would be an appropriate time to end this arrangement, putting citizens of the Irish Republic on a par with those of any other foreign country in the EU. Then, in logic and in fairness, the same attitude could be taken to the Scots, who must learn – as must the Irish – that they cannot have their constitutional cake and eat it. Many Scots, whether resident in England or not, may well want to take English citizenship, once such a status exists. Their applications will no doubt be looked upon favourably. Since Scotland and England are both likely to remain members of the EU, free transit between the two countries is likely to continue. It is not even certain that there will have to be border posts at Gretna and Berwick, though that will depend greatly on what immigration policies the newly independent Scotland chooses to operate. If its doors are to be open to all manner of people that England would not wish to entertain for economic reasons, then clearly controls will be necessary.

It may be argued, by peers as well as by proletarians, that as Scotland is likely to share a monarchy with England, all this talk of separate citizenships is somewhat extreme. Well, England shares a monarchy with Australia – indeed, shares ties of blood with Australia closer in many cases than those it shares with Scotland – and that cuts little ice with English immigration officers. Australians may have the same Queen, and in many cases be of British ethnic origins, but they have no right to work or settle in what is presently the United Kingdom. It is often helpful if they can find, say, an Italian grandmother or a Greek grandfather, as this can get them citizenship of those countries, and the right to enter, settle and work in Britain as EU nationals. The Scots will at least be EU nationals: as such, under the Treaty of Maastricht, they may vote at local (but not at parliamentary) elections. However, it is quite right that any Scot who wishes to participate either in the English parliament or at English parliamentary elections should, first, become an English citizen. This may be troublesome for the Scots concerned, but at least the origins of the problem will not be of England's making.

V

The challenge for the English, in the event of these circumstances coming to pass, would be to forge a nationalism that, while respecting and advancing the aspirations of the English, does not contribute to xenophobic feelings among the inhabitants of these islands for each other. However hard or unlikely this may seem, this can be done only by a clean break with Scotland – and, belatedly, with the Republic of Ireland. Each constituent part of the former kingdom has to be aware of where it stands in relation to the others, and that will necessitate a new deal between the respective countries. This, perhaps, is another use for the SNP's much-vaunted 'Association of British States', a possible forum in which the basic philosophy of the new separatism can be thrashed out. It means accepting, on all sides, that with proper independence comes proper responsibility. It means that if England is to be removed from having control or influence over the affairs of other parts of the Kingdom that now not only consider themselves distinct, but which have taken legal moves to enforce their distinctness, then England is no longer required to provide any sort of financial or social support to those territories, nor to allow other nationals a say in the government of England.

In this day and age, though, it would not be such political considerations that dominated the question of how England's relations ought to be with Scotland if the Union were dissolved. Economics would be a principal concern. It is not in England's interests to have a bankrupt neighbour, especially one with which it shares a land border. There is a belief among some in Scotland that England has somehow exploited Scotland economically, and that independence should be accompanied by a dowry of some sort, paid by England to the Scots, signifying the end of an imaginary, moral economic debt. This notion has no basis in fact, but that will not prevent certain Scots from seeking to extract moral blackmail. Nor will it prevent some in England from suggesting that some sort of aid programme – rather as Britain has conducted towards undeveloped countries in the third world – should be mounted 'on a transitional basis' for the benefit of Scotland. In the interests of a harmonious relationship between England and Scotland it is essential that independence marks the end of any financial claim that either country might have on the other. If not, then resentment is bound to fester, despite the close social and cultural ties that will continue to exist, and despite the two countries possibly even sharing the same monarch.

The question remains of the national debt. Entertaining though the prospect is, it would not be so simple as to divide the debt by each head of the population in the United Kingdom, and present the Scots with a bill for their share. There would be endless arguments about the uses to which the expenditure that incurred the debt was put. It would be contended, not entirely accurately, that England had been a disproportionate beneficiary of past spending, notably that arising out of the two world wars. Even if actuaries could prove down to the last penny the level of Scotland's indebtedness, it is out of the question that Scotland could afford to pay it back to England, any more than England, if presented with a demand for its own debt tomorrow, could repay its creditors. It is, however, unrealistic for the Scots to expect to be a nation without debt, or at least without a debt to service: there is no reason why they should be given a free gift of that order. An arrangement would need to be reached, therefore, where some sort of notional interest payment was made to the English Treasury in recognition of the fact of England's bearing Scotland's historic debts. If the Scots say that this is unfair (which it manifestly would not be), then they should be firmly reminded that paying one's way, and settling one's debts, are indispensable accoutrements of a grown-up, independent country. If it wishes to be taken seriously in Europe, as opposed to being patronised as an outpost of the third world in the northern hemisphere, Scotland cannot choose to dine *à la carte* at the table of nationhood.

The more a climate can be created in which neither the English nor the Scots are given cause to resent each other, the better. Given the likely cooperation in matters of defence, the sharing of a monarchy and the high proportion of trade that Scotland does with England – not to mention the obvious ties of language, history and culture – there is likely to be plenty of common ground on which the two countries could meet. The Association of British States, or something like it, would be a forum in which good relations could be established; and there would need to be frequent bilateral meetings between English and Scottish ministers, as matters with potential for mis-understanding – such as the respective countries' immigration policies – would be likely to crop up regularly. In practical terms, there is likely to be no alternative to a special relationship between England and Scotland; the inevitable, and welcome, consequence of two countries that ought to be united choosing to go their separate ways.

Should Scotland become independent, it would be at liberty to manage all aspects of its internal and external affairs as it saw fit. This would be sure to lead, in time, to variances from the policies adopted by Great Britain. There would, of course, be the constraint of both countries' membership of the European Union, and possible membership of the same defence pact, to keep Scottish and English policies on a broadly parallel course. However, Scotland could choose externally to pursue close relations with countries that England prefers to keep at arm's length, or vice versa. In an age when economic rivalry has replaced armed conflict as the most usual means of contention between nations, both countries' conduct of foreign policy would be likely to be influenced most substantially by trading considerations.

England, however, with its greater weight in the world, might like to take the opportunity of such a new dawn to consider the very basis of its own foreign policy. The cession of Scotland from the Union would be the most fundamental act of non-imperialism. It might, therefore, be time for the first English foreign secretary to strip out of his policy all those relics of England as an imperial power. There would need to be a fresh statement of what, exactly, English interests were. There could be an assessment not just of how well England is equipped to undertake the role that Britain these days sometimes finds so attractive – that of assistant world policeman in America's international constabulary – but how desirable it is that England should undertake it. Nothing is more shocking to the English sensibility than the notion that the country might, when evil is being done abroad, pass by on the other side. Memories are too fresh of the 1930s, when Hitler was persecuting Jews and political opponents a few hundred miles from London, while England did all it could to make that persecution no more difficult than it had to be. This shameful memory has been partly why Britain has been so keen to be involved in taming gangster states in the Middle East, or of disciplining savages in the Balkans, even though no British national interest has been proved to be at stake.

The reconstituting of the English foreign office would be an ideal time to reaffirm basic English values of humanity, democracy and fairness. It would also be worth defining those countries in whose affairs England has a need or right to take a close interest, and those in whose it does not. Those nations with whom we are in formal alliance, either through NATO or the EU, clearly come into the first category. So too do countries with which England has strong historic ties, or ties of blood; though it would also be a good opportunity for England to work out whether the Commonwealth, which is principally an English operation in terms of its funding and organisation and for which England provides the head, is the right medium through which to be conducting relationships with former colonies. England ought to stress, though, that having a legitimate right to be actively interested in a country is not the same as it being acceptable to intervene in its internal, or external, affairs. That can only be right when an English national interest is at stake, which is why we need to be told what they are.

Obviously, England needs to be concerned with the stability and conduct of countries with whom it does significant amounts of trade. The murky waters of the so-called 'ethical foreign policy' need to be avoided. In a free market economy such as Britain is and England would be, the moral judgment about trading with a country whose record on, say, human rights is unpleasant needs to be made by those consumers who must, in the end, decide whether or not to open their wallets. That is different, though, from an English foreign secretary fawning upon dictators and other undesirables, in the way that, for example, Douglas Hurd did on the Chinese so soon after the murders in Tiananmen Square. Trading with countries while regarding them as morally unacceptable is not hypocrisy: it is good business. After all, individuals buy products all the time from merchants with whom they would not dream of having a social relationship. It is the same with nations. If the English foreign office could restore such a clear sense of what England stands for in the world, and how exactly it intends to stand for it, then it would make the most of the opportunity presented by the fresh start.

It would be important for the English foreign office to tell the world by word and example, with what sort of country they would be dealing. This might be a very similar country to the Britain that has been superseded: but it would do no harm to say so. It would be hard to counter the obsession among the English political class with the notion of how their country is perceived in the world, so it might be as well to give the world a little guidance. Other than proclaiming the continuity of English values as a force for good internationally, it would be important for the foreign office to announce two other things to the world: that Scottish independence will do nothing to harm England or her allies strategically, and that as an economic force England would be a stronger and more efficient entity than Britain was capable of being.

In domestic policy, the English government would have little reason to change much of what already pertains. The end of the requirement to subsidise Scotland would increase the disposable income of the English, if the government of the day chose to pass the windfall back to them. It might decide that such a burst of liquidity in England would be inflationary, so it might instead use the money to repay part of the national debt. The English have taken well to the economics of the last twenty years, when attempts have been made to increase disposable income and reduce the size and scope of the state. The Scots did not like it, as we have noted, and it has been one of the factors that has driven the Conservatives in Scotland into oblivion, and which threatens to damage Labour there. The English way would seem to be a continued reduction in the size of the state, an encouragement of individual prosperity and self-reliance, and the further development of a culture of commercial risk and wealth creation of a sort that has, apparently, become anathematical to the Scots. It would depend on what sort of government ran an independent England, and it would depend too on the development of regional consciousness. In the end, though, an English parliament would be able to tailor all its policies specifically to the demands of the English citizen – so far as it was allowed to do so by the European Union. It might well be that independence for England also provides the impetus for a reconsideration of the long-term nature of its relationship with the EU, and a close look at the balance sheet to decide what, exactly, the benefits are of English membership of this cartel. It is certainly another one of those debates that the English must have among themselves when and if independence is achieved, especially in the light of Europe developing along socialist lines that are anathematical to the English spirit, and even to much of what now calls itself the English Labour party.

VI

The present Labour government has made a fetish out of constitutional reform. It has argued that many existing British institutions do not work and need to be altered, such as the Union itself, the House of Lords and the voting system. There has also been a climate – not, it seems, entirely coincidental – in which it has become usual to accept that the monarchy must be reformed too. This desire for reform and the high proportion of the government that is Scottish may not be coincidental either. Certainly, Scotland was the one distinct part of the United Kingdom where there was a loud call for constitutional change – which has now been granted. The English have shown far less enthusiasm for change, an outlook that could be dismissed as being all part of their general uninterest in politics. It is also, though, attributable to the fact that most of the English feel their institutions work perfectly well, and that dissatisfaction with them is the concern purely of those in ivory towers with nothing better to do. It is salutary to note how the government's vendetta against the predominantly English institution of the House of Lords has been conducted without any feeling among the English people that there is any pressing need to reform that institution.

The general satisfaction that the English feel with their institutions would seem to suggest that, while there may be cause for the government of a newly independent England to make various statements of general policy, there is unlikely to be any real need for it to spend time, money and energy rebuilding the machinery of government. What would be necessary would be a reaffirmation through the English parliament of the validity of other English institutions and parts of the English constitution – notably the monarchy, the peerage, the judiciary and local government. An English government could also attempt to tackle an issue that British governments have failed to control for decades: the very size of the state. If English anti-statism is to be furthered by an English government, then reductions in the size of the government itself, of the Civil Service, and of the bureaucracy ought to be attempted.

It would also be useful for the English if their parliament took practical steps to rebuild the national identity in just the way that, as we have seen, the Scots propose to do: by harnessing a distinct and vibrant national culture to which the majority of English, and not just a sectarian elite, can relate. Institutions and culture are together important because of what they mean for national self-confidence, and the projection of a nation in the world. The revived English parliament would play a key part in this exercise, as would the English government: both institutions would be focuses of the new, positive spirit of England, and both would lay the foundations for England's achievement in the years after independence. They would need to help devise and support the cultural projects, in schools, in the arts, in broadcasting and elsewhere, that would project the English temper, English attitudes and the English way of life both to the English people and to the world. In practical terms, this would entail taking that leaf out of the SNP's book. Scotland has never been embarrassed about itself; it is time for the English to think likewise.

Education policy would be at the heart of this project in England, just as the SNP intends it to be in Scotland. It would mean teaching English culture in schools – not just English literature, but English music, art and, of course, English history. There can be no question of such teaching taking the anti-intellectual approach of professing some sort of superiority for this culture: what it must do is stress both its distinctness and its connection with the European mainstream. Nor should it be retrospective: it is vital that, as part of England's new identity, the writers, composers, artists, architects and designers of the twenty-first century should be seen in the continuum that contains Chaucer, Tallis, Constable, Henry Yevele and Inigo Jones. More modern forms of expression, such as cinema, must be encouraged too: seldom has the nature of England and English life been expressed so vividly as in the English cinema of the 1940s, before the industry declined into almost unrelieved second-rateness. It has picked up again in recent years and is the model of the diverse, yet distinct, cultural flavour that England today can have.

Given the present popularity of London internationally as a centre of fashion and culture, such a programme of cultural revival and expression should have a great impetus behind it. This may sound unpleasantly, to some, like the present government's bizarre 'Cool Britannia' project. It would, however, have certain important differences from that enterprise. First, it would be about England, not Britain. Second, it would not have 'Cool Britannia's' fetish for ignoring, writing off or discounting the past – quite the reverse, as there would need to be a conscious atavism in order to confirm the long traditions of culture in this country and the nourishment those traditions should give to creative Englishmen and women today. Third, it would not be a party political or commercial exercise of the sort that 'Cool Britannia' has been seen to be, but one with the general and (it is to be hoped) non-controversial aim of raising the awareness of the English about their own culture, and raising the profile of English culture in the world.

Apart from doing this through the school curriculum, thereby trying to ensure that future generations are not so ignorant of their country's cultural achievements in the broadest sense as recent ones have been, there are other means the government can take to further these aims. There is, for example, the matter of the disbursement of funds to the Arts Council. Much of this money is already used to encourage native talent, if with inadequate quality control. Means should be devised to encourage not just English artists and performers, but the creation and performance of English works – whether music, drama or film. If public subsidy continues to be paid to artists and performers in England – and at a time when some sort of identity needs to be created, it would seem sensible to do so, despite the formidable ideological objections to such subsidy – then it would seem sensible to use more of it to promote English culture, both by encouraging creativity and performance, and taking the national culture, past and present, into schools. Coordinating such a programme would seem, at last, to provide something serious for the Department of Culture to do. That department would, though, need to undergo a culture change of its own, being more geared to the promotion of what England has to offer.

As for broadcasting, a distinction must be drawn between the public service channels and those in the commercial sector. Some European countries impose quotas governing the per-centage of home-made programmes that have to be shown on a particular network. It would be fundamentally illiberal, not to mention potentially commercially disastrous, to tell the private sector that it had to fill up its afternoons with English rather than Australian and American soap operas. It is not in the country's interests to make broadcasting an uncommercial activity. However, the BBC, funded as it is by public money, has different responsibilities. The question of the future of the British Broadcasting Corporation once there ceases to be a Britain is one that must in any case be resolved. The Scots would want control of their own public service broadcaster. The division of the BBC into English and Scottish businesses should be straightforward, given the regional nature of much that the Corporation does. There are already dedicated news programmes and other services provided by the BBC for Scot-land. The SBC (or whatever it was called) would no doubt angle its programming towards its own local cultural interests, and it would make sense for the EBC to do the same. The

EBC's programmes might well be available in Scotland – just as the BBC's are now in the Republic of Ireland – but there would be no cause to take into account a Scottish audience when making programmes.

In terms of news coverage, the EBC would have no need to be any more insular than the BBC currently is. Nor should there be great implications for any other part of its output, with one exception. That exception must be the performing arts. For example, the BBC uses the public's money to promote the annual Henry Wood Promenade Concerts. There have been arguments in the past about the composition of these programmes, given what has been seen to be the BBC's duty to promote British music. In fact, each Proms season includes a number of newly commissioned works from native composers, as well as a decent smattering of music from the established English repertoire. The EBC should be required to satisfy the Department of Culture that its musical output – popular as well as classical – gives weight to English artists and composers. So long as it is raising money from the English people to provide this service in the name of the English state – and whether it should continue to do so or not ought to be a debate that the English should have among themselves at an early juncture in their independence – then it must expect to be required to take upon itself the duty of promoting the English performing arts. After all, if it does not do so, there is unlikely to be any other country that will step in and do it instead. Similarly, English playwrights, living and dead, should feature prominently in radio and television drama output: not to the exclusion of foreign ones, but in sufficient profusion to raise cultural consciousness. To judge from the BBC's current output, this would not require much of a departure from the norm. On television, the EBC should complement the patronage of English dramatists that it would inherit from the BBC by becoming involved in the revival of the English cinema; something in which Channel Four has led the way since its foundation in 1982.

Those who fear English nationalism for its supposed aggressive or chauvinistic potential should take heart from any attempt to ensure that in its new incarnation it is seen as being predominantly culturally based. There will always be those who choose to express their nationality in disgusting ways; they choose to do it now before there is an independent England, and they will be sure to do it if England becomes independent. If a movement can be created for the expression of Englishness by pacific and unthreatening means, such people will always remain at the margins of the largely civilised society in which they live. Similarly, an England in which cherished traditions of justice, tolerance and the rule of law are to be paramount must ensure that those who engage in profoundly antisocial behaviour that threatens to undermine the benign and respectable image of England are treated not just with disdain, but with severity. Once it has been established that the new England is above all a civilised country, there need be no questions about its place in the world, of its suitability as an ally or business partner.

VII

Of course, none of this may come about. Scotland may pull back from the brink. What looks now to be an inevitable course, what seems to be the compulsion on the part of the Scottish people to experiment with independence, may go into reverse. The English, as so often, may choose to tolerate what any other country would regard as the intolerable – funding a territory whose domestic policies and politicians are not accountable to the assembly that provides it with most of its money. Millions of old romantics on both sides of the border will be hoping, as the first Scottish elections take place, that such an apocalypse cannot be possible. Even if the SNP comes to form an administration, the romantics will not believe that the people of

Scotland could possibly, once the argument is properly had out, choose to sunder their country from England.

Yet the likelihood is that this is an argument that will not go away, whatever the outcome of the May 1999 elections. The Scots have too large a force in their population that wants to taste the dish of independence; and as this is an infection that spreads mainly among the young, it is growing. The English are becoming steadily more aware of Scotland's preferential treatment. If this growing awareness does not lead to their being asked a direct question about the link with Scotland, it is sure to encourage one of the main political parties – most likely the Conservatives – to develop policies that amount to the same thing. Just as the Scots have thought hard (but not necessarily well) for decades about what independence would mean to them, so too would the English start to think about what it could mean for them. That seems to be the inevitable consequence of the existing, unfair arrangements for devolution. Whereas the Scots can only come to the view that their nation would be viable as an independent state by recourse to fantasy, the English can feel that about themselves without stretching the imagination at all.

Although England has long been good in battle – lately, it must be admitted, with great help from the Scots – it has rarely excelled at making the important political decisions that must precede any sort of action. What happened in the 1930s was not an aberration in that regard, but a glowing demonstration of the weakness and stupidity of the English establishment. If Scotland goes, England will have to make one of the great choices in its history: a choice of returning to the sort of international self-assertion it practised easily and successfully before 1707, or of failing to rise to the challenge of its new independence by surrendering to absorption into the European superstate. Here, there is a lesson for England in the re-emergence of the nations of eastern Europe after the Soviet hegemony from 1945 to 1990. The only difference is that England is equipped by her wealth, populousness and established international contacts to become the ultimate success as a 'new nation', catching a tide of history that has been flowing strongly since the coming down of the Iron Curtain and which celebrates a resurgent, constructive nationalism. As with those new nations of eastern Europe, England too can take its place in the civilised world, its national identity a source of strength and pride rather than an embarrassment.

Finally, we must be aware that nothing is forever, and it is far from certain that the event of 1707 was unique in history. For the first few years of an independent Scotland the deficit caused by losing the financial support of the English taxpayer would doubtless be made up by Europe, in the interests of Brussels acquiring a new and loyal client state and preserving stability in the region. Yet that kind of support cannot possibly continue indefinitely. Scotland will have to make a success of its own economy, and pay its own way. If it loses its best brains and best businesses through high taxation, it could quickly find itself reduced to the level of a cold-weather theme park. It was economic failure before that forced Scotland into the arms of the English: and it is far from certain that such circumstances might not come about again. Some years in the future, the Scots themselves might see that it is once more in Scotland's interests to unite with the English. If and when that time comes, the English will need to consider the prospects on a purely commercial basis. The new English nation that must be forged must, if it is to prosper, be one as free as possible from the meaningless trappings of sentiment. The new English will be first and foremost a mercantile people, whose relations with the world are those primarily of a business partner. This is not Little Englandism: it is simply an observance of the realities that England's financial predicament would dictate. Fundamentally, the end of the Union would be the time for an audit of all England's aspirations, and for the imposition of a salutary objectivity about its place in the world.

The English have every reason to believe that this can be a

prosperous and constructive future in which England is a force for good, moderation and sanity, and in which the English state serves first and foremost the interests of the English people; but it requires a recognition of the true condition of England, and of the need to create a national identity for the English again. We can either leave that task to the modern Jingoists, with their following of spiky-haired louts with red and white faces, or the civilised and educated classes who have so long repudiated and cringed at the very idea of nationalism can take a hand in creating a more acceptable form of it themselves. There is the problem that many in this class no longer feel that England should have its own interests, or identity, but that these should be submerged in the interests and supposed identity of a larger, multi-national state. In this, to judge from the resistance of the British people to ideas of European integration as displayed in opinion polls, such elements of the political class are not reflecting popular feeling.

In the end, a constructive, peaceful nationalism, with the re-creation of national identity and the reinvention of England as an independent and proud nation, is something that would be likely to command the support of a majority of English people. They would see it as making the best of a decision by Scotland to fracture the Union, and a happy and positive alternative to wailing and gnashing of teeth. It is they, still, as Chesterton put it, 'that have never spoken yet'. It is a fundamental democratic offence that the English have not themselves been consulted about how they see their future, and any government that believes in fairness should ask them. If that fundamental right continues to be denied the English, and if, instead, Scotland should speak for them, then the Scots could well take the decision to make England independent. If that should happen, then the least the English people have a right to expect is that their governors – as the custodians both of their history and of their future – will have the right idea of what to do, and the confidence to do it.